CW01664044

MABEL BRAILSFORD

A wartime journal
1941 to 1943

First published in 2016 by
Amersham Museum
49 High Street, Amersham,
Buckinghamshire, HP7 0DP.
www.amershammuseum.org
www.amershamhistory.info

Company registration No. 1790935
Charity registration No. 288865

Copyright © 2016 by Amersham Museum.

All rights reserved.
No part of this publication may be used or reproduced in any manner whatsoever without the written permission of Amersham Museum, except in the case of brief excerpts embodied in critical articles and reviews.

Every effort has been made to contact copyright holders; any omissions are inadvertent and will be corrected in future editions if notification of the amended credit is sent to the publisher in writing.

Additional material and edited by Wendy Tibbitts.

Design by Danny Robins.

Printed in Great Britain by Book Printing UK.

Bodytype set in 10/14 Minion Pro.

ISBN 978-1-5262-0247-5

index

Amersham Museum is indebted to memories of Miss Brailsford from Methodist Church members, Mr and Mrs Stratfull of Amersham. Mr George Bunney and Mrs Ann Mills shared their reminiscences of the Music Studio. For memories of Mabel's friend Emily Bolam and background to some of the events mentioned in the journal we are grateful to Mr Godfrey Bolam. Some of the family photos are part of the archive of H.N. Brailsford held at the People's History Museum in Manchester, to whom Amersham Museum is indebted for their assistance.

Amersham Museum wishes to thank the Abbeyfield Society for permission to reproduce this work. It is also grateful for permissions received from the National Trust, The People's Dispensary for Sick Animals, and the National Children's Homes.

introduction

At the height of the Second World War Winston Churchill said, *"This is no time for ease and comfort. It is time to dare and endure."* There is no doubt that the people of Britain did 'endure' not just on the battlefield, but in their streets and homes. The war touched everyone's lives. What was it like to live with the wartime deprivations, the upheavals and anxieties? Fortunately some personal histories exist that enable us to have an insight into life at that time.

Such a history has been donated to Amersham Museum in the form of three slim handwritten notebooks discovered in the drawer of a table bought at auction in Norfolk. The purchaser, recognizing the association with Amersham, kindly donated them to the Museum. The notebooks contain a journal kept by an author documenting her life between 1941 and 1943. She described national events and personalities, war-damaged London, deprivations, personal stories of friends and neighbours, the problems of living with evacuees, as well as recording the people and events in Amersham, Buckinghamshire. This book presents a transcription of her notebooks, alongside some letters and ephemera she had inserted in them, and gives us a fascinating glimpse into her life and thoughts during those wartime years.

The writer was Miss Mabel Richmond Brailsford 1875–1970 who, at that time, lived in Greylands, London Road East, Amersham, Buckinghamshire. She shared her home with her elderly Mother, and some bombed-out evacuees from London. Mabel was 65. She was well-educated and a published author of historical biographies. A list of her published work and her biography are included in this volume, but the main interest is her account of daily life in wartime Britain.

The journal contains her opinions and prejudices about people she knew and met. She clearly had favourites, and others she described more harshly. She expressed her opinions freely – some of it kindly and amusing, some of it acerbic or uninformed gossip, but all of it revealing of her character, and her social background. She used words in an interesting yet archaic way, and mixes in Italian, Spanish, German, French and Latin phrases. Where possible these have been translated to make her thoughts meaningful. She clearly wanted to express her feelings and her journal gave her an outlet.

Sometimes the journal is an essay of Mabel's views on a particular subject, and sometimes she appears to be writing specifically for a reader. This reader was her profoundly deaf Mother. It is thought that originally there were more volumes of the journal as each of the notebooks in the Museum's possession start at the top of the first page and continued to the bottom of the last page. The last volume ends just before her Mother's hundredth birthday, and leaves us with a burning desire to know more.

Mabel wrote: *"this record has been little but a private diary and of no interest as a sidelight on the War."* It seems that she had intended to chronicle life in wartime Britain but it had become more personal. Whatever her motivation in writing the journal, she probably did not expect it to be read and published 70 years later. There are over 150 people and places mentioned in the journal and all have been individually researched and described in more detail in an appendix. The journal opens with an accommodation crisis in their home, caused by what she calls her *"horrible sense of duty"* in giving over two of the three bedrooms to evacuees who have been bombed out of their London homes.

biography

Mabel Richmond Brailsford

1875 – 1970

"I think my life is rather like a book ... it is lived in isolated chapters, differing totally in atmosphere and content with only the one slender connection that all the events happen to the same person."
Mabel Brailsford, April 1943

It seems fitting that an author of historical biographies should think of her life in the form of chapters of a book. Her life spanned a period of significant changes. Born a Victorian, but living through three-quarters of the twentieth century we learn from her journal how her upbringing coloured her opinions and shaped her character.

Noel, Clara and Mabel, circa 1877

Mabel Richmond Brailsford was born on 22 November 1875 in Mirfield, Yorkshire into a household of Victorian gentility. Mabel's middle name was derived from her Father's Grandmother, Richmond Exley, who was living with the family at the time of the census in 1881.

Her Father, Edward John Brailsford, was a Wesleyan Methodist Minister, from Birmingham. He had been described as *"the poet preacher of Wesleyan Methodism"* for his stylish sermons. [1] Clara, Mabel's mother, was born in Liverpool, the eighth of eleven children of wealthy industrialist Henry Pooley. The Pooley family were devout Wesleyan Methodists and philanthropists.

Rev. Brailsford's devotion to his church work made him a distant figure in Mabel's life. Her Mother had the dual role of assisting her husband in his Ministry and managing the household. Mabel and her older brother, Henry Noel, were mainly brought up by servants and relied on each other for companionship. [2] Edward Brailsford's Methodist Ministry required the family to relocate around Britain every few years, which made it difficult for Mabel to form any childhood friendships. In a Victorian class-conscious society Mabel's lifelong shyness was not helped by a feeling of disconnection from any particular social strata. As a Minister's daughter she was expected to be aloof from close contact with the working classes, but being a Methodist also excluded her from the local social elite. It is probable that she had no close friends of her own age until she went to 'Wintersdorf' a Methodist girls' boarding school in Birkdale, Lancashire.

1 The United Methodist. 9 Aug 1917.

2 Leventhal, F.M. The Last Dissenter, Clarendon Press, Oxford. 2003 p9.

Mabel excelled at school. At the age of 15 she successfully passed the Cambridge Local Examinations with 2nd class honours. She passed in religious knowledge, English, German, drawing and music with a distinction in French. [3] Sadly, after finishing at boarding school, she was not given the opportunity to go to University like her elder Brother. Apart from occasional courses in German Literature in Queen Margaret's college, Edinburgh, and a six month educational stay in Berlin, Mabel had a lifelong role as her Mother's companion and never married. However she did write some well regarded historical biographies of religious figures, and translated two non-fiction books from German into English. (See page 133 for a Bibliography).

Some of Mabel Brailsford's biographies were of the Wesley family, but her best-known book is about William Penn.[4] She wrote several books about Quaker leaders, carrying out her research in the archives of Friends House, London, and forming friendships from within the community of the Society of Friends. On moving to Buckinghamshire she frequently attended meetings at the Amersham Meeting House.[5]

Mabel with a group of convalescing officers, Woolacombe Bay, 1918.

3 The Dundee Courier and Argus, Wednesday 23 April 1890.
4 Brailsford, Mabel Richmond. The Making of William Penn, Longmans, Green & Co. (London, 1930)
5 From an interview with Godfrey Bolam, son of the warden of Amersham Friends House.

Mabel, third from the left, bottom row. Watermouth Castle, Ilfracombe.

Her Father, Edward Brailsford's last Methodist Circuit was at Ilfracombe in Devon. At the start of the Great War Mabel was writing *Quaker Woman* which was published in 1915.[6] In August the following year her Father retired from his full-time ministry and Mabel began war work with the Voluntary Aid Detachment. Photographs from the family archive show her wearing the uniform of a VAD official. In one photo she is shyly sitting with a group of convalescing officers on the beach at nearby Woolacombe Bay in February 1918, and another photo shows her sitting sideways, bottom left, with the nursing staff of the VAD hospital at Watermouth Castle, Ilfracombe.

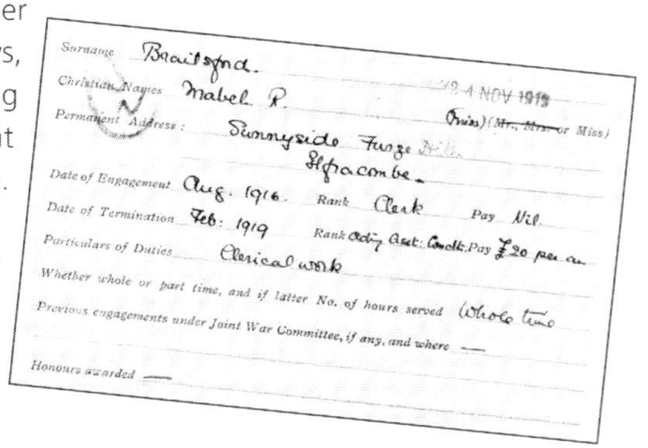

Surname Brailsford.
Christian Names Mabel R. 4 NOV 1919
Permanent Address: Sunnyside Furze Hill Ilfracombe. (Miss) (~~Mr., Mrs~~ or Miss)
Date of Engagement Aug. 1916. Rank Clerk Pay Nil.
Date of Termination Feb: 1919 Rank Acting Asst: Comdt. Pay £20 per an
Particulars of Duties Clerical work
Whether whole or part time, and if latter No. of hours served Whole time
Previous engagements under Joint War Committee, if any, and where —
Honours awarded —

Official Red Cross records show that she worked there full-time for nearly three years and rose from being a clerk to Acting Assistant Commandant.

6 Brailsford, Mabel Richmond. *Quaker Women*, 1650 – 1690. Duckworth (London, 1915)

After her Father's death in 1921, aged 80, Mabel and her Mother, Clara, moved to Amersham, Buckinghamshire. Her brother, Noel, was only a short train-ride away in Hampstead. When they first arrived in Amersham they lived at Little Elms, London Road East, but later moved a few houses along to Greylands. Greylands was a three-bedroomed bungalow surrounded by a large garden. It overlooked the picturesque Misbourne valley, but was a little isolated from the town. Mabel travelled everywhere on her basket-fronted bicycle, and as we read in her journal, frequently cycled to Amersham-on-the-Hill for the train station or the Music Studio. This entailed riding up an arduously steep hill and returning home down the hill in the blackout.

Mabel contributed to the Amersham community by playing the piano for the services at the Methodist Church in Amersham. A member of the congregation remembers, as a small boy, being fascinated by her use of strategically mounted elastic on the hem of her skirt which she used to secure her skirt to her legs whilst cycling. [7] She had a great love of music and her journal tells of her delight at attending the concerts and lectures in the Music Studio. The Nobel Prize-winning writer, Elias Canetti, who met Mabel at the Music Studio, described her as, *"A small, frail, very ancient woman, with a wobbling head."* [8] She described him as "quite young, eager looking with [a] typical German face." In fact he was originally from Bulgaria.

Mabel and her Mother lived at Greylands until their deaths. Clara died in 1944 at the age of 101, but Mabel's role as nurse and companion did not end there. In 1952 her brother, H.N. Brailsford, the left-wing writer and broadcaster, moved in with her and once again they enjoyed the companionship of their childhood. Mabel nursed her brother, and his weak heart, at Greylands for the last six years of his life, until he died in 1958.

7 Interview with Gerald Stratfull.

8 Canetti, Elias. Party in the Park, The Harvill Press. (London, 2005) p.75

Mabel outlived her Brother by a further 12 years. It is hoped that her final years were comfortable. She had a live-in companion/carer for the last few years of her life, which she acknowledged with a substantial legacy in her Will. She died at the age of 94 in Chesham Cottage hospital on 26th April 1970, of pneumonia, heart failure, and suffering from arthritis and Parkinsonism. The informant on her death certificate was the undertaker. So little was known about her that her date of birth was recorded as unknown. In her Will she showed her love for Amersham by leaving a legacy to the Abbeyfield Society who purchased a house in Plantation Road, Amersham for six elderly residents, and called it Brailsford House. She also left legacies to the PDSA, the National Trust, the National Children's Homes, and the Guild of Aid for Gentle People, as well as Mr and Mrs Burrows who feature in her journal.

Mabel had a long and active life. She devoted it to the service of her family and although her writing was published and well-received, her domestic duties prevented her from achieving her full potential as a writer. Her biographies have given pleasure to many. This publication should be her memorial.

Brailsford House, Amersham, was sold and is now a private residence.

Monday July 14, 1941

The Billeting Officer has just been here. The Lewises had called on him – very decent of them to do it at once. But he has no hope whatever of getting them another billet and begged us to go on. He was shocked at the idea of them going nearer London, since they had been kept safe for nearly a year and there might be a new Blitz at any time. He entirely sympathises with us and was very sorry. Miss Barnes gave a vague threat that she wouldn't stay, but believe she will think better of it. She was very disappointed and very cross.

I am going in September to move this couch into the sitting room – and sleep on it – the wove is spoiled already so it doesn't matter. The one thing I am determined on is that we shall both sleep peacefully – when it gets too cold for me to be on the verandah.

Stamford Hill [1] – I suggested that [2] and she poured out a spate of lying excuses that it was impossible. I expect the eldest son won't have them. She would get it so dirty.

Tuesday July 15, 1941

St Swithin's day and very showery – Morning in War time.
I was due at the Dentists at 11.30am. Of course I walked up Station Hill after a bit: but before I got off [3] I overtook two girls carrying a very heavy basket. They were most grateful when I suggested putting it on the back carrier and wheeling it up. They had come from Oxford this morning, hitch hiking all the way, and a lorry had brought them to the foot of Station Hill. They thought they were on their way to Chorley Wood so I advised them to take the train – it is only the second station on this line. It was a nice little episode and I arrived in good time at Mr Wege's. [4] I thought he looked dead tired so I asked him how they were getting on as Mrs Wege has had such difficulty in finding help. "*Very badly*" he said. She can get no help at all. The minute a woman comes to interview her she sees the big house and hears there are three children and nothing will persuade her to come. They also have hens and ducks. On his way home he has to call at the Soldiers' Canteen for

1 Where the Lewis's son lives.
2 That the Lewises should move there.
3 Mabel rode everywhere on her bicycle.
4 The Dentist.

Wege & MacGillivray Dental Surgery

scraps and all that has to be cooked. He helps in the house at the end of his days' work and they never get to bed before twelve. He said, half in fun, that if things went on like this he would have to leave his practice and stay at home to do the housework.

I thought perhaps Mrs Coleman would condescend to go for a couple of hours till they could find someone to live in and I thought Emily Bolam might know a German refugee to whom it would be a godsend. So I called at both places on the way home. There is a Committee Meeting tomorrow dealing with refugees and she will put the matter before them. But Mrs Coleman wouldn't go. I thought perhaps you [5] would like to help her with the childrens' socks?

Monday July 21, 1941

9 Fern Close, Welwyn Garden City. I came here on Saturday for a long weekend with Lucy. I have been anxious to see London before it was put to rights and I am not sorry I did, but it was a heart rending experience. The Green Line Coaches are no longer running between Amersham and London – they were converted into ambulances. Old London buses (two deckers) are used instead and I can travel in them with impunity, as smoking is allowed only on the upper deck and there is plenty of air in the lower. The windows however are covered with some kind of coarse green net, glued on, with only a tiny space left free. I had a front seat and could look out from behind the driver, when I raised myself on Miss Barnes' suitcase. I had been intending to take my very shabby blue one, as I have lent Mr Lewis the respectable hide one I had from Windy Knowe [6]. But Miss Barnes insisted on lending me a similar one belonging to herself – at the same time throwing out very strong hints in Mrs Lewis' presence, that I ought to have the use of my own. They produced no effect however and I never

5 Mabel's mother, Clara, was deaf and read this journal.

6 Windy Knowe, is the name of the house in Wells, Somerset where her cousin Mab Keogh lived. Mabel inherited the residue of her estate in 1935.

know how much or how little Mrs Lewis takes in. I am afraid Miss Barnes does pursue a policy of pinpricks towards her and I don't like it – I should wish her to be happy as long as she is in our house, quite irrespective of her desserts – well to continue. There was no sign of the war all the way, except for a very few houses demolished or with windows broken. The Shepherds Bush Cinema however, was in ruins – it used to be an opera house where Lucy took me once from Charleville Mansions to see the Beggars Opera. I got out at Marble Arch and tried then to find out where the Welwyn Garden City coaches started from – but neither taxi driver nor policeman could tell me. So I left it, and set myself to getting rid of the case while I went sightseeing. I tried to leave it at Marble Arch Station but left luggage is no longer accepted there and they told me the nearest place was Oxford Circus. This was on the route, so I got a bus down Oxford Street for 1½d – all penny fares are abolished. We passed on the left John Lewis' huge building – now only a mass of rubble, with a few girders protruding from the heap. I had to ask a good many directions during the morning and I found everyone most helpful and interested – far more leisured and less keyed up, it seemed to me, than they used to be in normal times. There was no sign of dislocation or distress or even of worry and haste. I walked down Wardour Street to the open air market recommended by Mrs Lewis, in search of a man's umbrella and a coarse set of china – but there were no such things on sale. At Marks and Spencer's I bought two very attractive sandwiches – lettuce tomato and cheese – and ordered a cup of coffee which I sat at a counter to consume – so a lunch much bigger than I could eat, cost me 6d. Then I caught the bus for St Pauls. We got as far as Trafalgar Square, with very little sign of damage – the lions were still there gazing over their paws as imperturbable as though no threat had come to England – and to my joy Nelson still stands on his slender column, unshaken by blast. Charles I, my best loved statue has been moved away, with his horse and Grinling Gibbons pedestal to a safe place in the country. Close to Charing Cross station there is a gaping hole where a shop or hotel once stood and received a bomb meant no doubt for the station – and poor St Clements Church stands on its island a gutted ruin, the tower and the walls alone remaining. Fleet Street had not suffered as I had expected – the damage I think was done in the quarters just behind the main frontage – The Manchester Guardian building was unharmed and from Fleet Street there was no sign of the desolation in the Temple. Then we came to the foot of Ludgate Hill and looked up to the miracle of the dome of St Pauls. It seemed to fling out a challenge almost insolent in its bravery. Beyond and at the side stood tottering walls, blackened timbers and windows emptied of glass. Great girders stood up drunkenly against the skyline and on the other side of the road a huge baulk of blackened timber showed where the fires had raged on that night of May 10. But St Pauls on the west side showed no sign of its ordeal, even Queen Anne seemed less dead than in the old days and stretched out her sceptre with an air of triumph. I went in at the West door and as I entered a pigeon flew across the Nave and rested at the top of one of the pillars. There was no sign of any hurt till one faced the east end and saw that the high altar was a heap of rubble, though the reredos still stands. It was not till I walked round outside to the East window that I realized how narrow had been St Paul's escape. Nothing but blackened walls is left of the huge building on the opposite side of the road, yet the fabric of St Pauls is unharmed in the sea of fire that must have raged around it. Only here and there great flakes of stone have fallen from the buttresses and all the glass has gone from the East window. For the first time since the war began my heart was hot with rage to think that this building so sacred and precious to everyone that speaks English had been exposed to such vile assault. Every day during the war there is Prayer from 1.05pm to 1.15pm in *"St Dunstans Chapel"* – a little side chapel on the left as one enters the side door. I went in and found about three females and two parsons. There had been a confirmation the day before and all the prayers were concerned with those who had just been confirmed and those who would *"make their first communion"* the following day. The only allusion to the War came in the end Collect for *"all soldiers sailors and airmen"*. It seemed a little inadequate, having regard to the scene outside. I went out again and sat under the blue sky, where two fat balloons [7] were shining in the sun, keeping watch over the City. At my feet were the remains of the

7 Barrage balloons were large tethered inflatables deployed over buildings to impede low-flying enemy aircraft.

Chapter House of old St Pauls, burnt down in 1666. I had the horrid fear that I was seeing new St Pauls for the last time and that on my next visit I should find nothing but a similar patch of labelled ruins. That glorious dome seems to offer an almost unmissable target, especially now that it rises unblemished out of a heap of ruins. Through all this the little border gardens round the walls are bright and tended, full of small begonias and dwarf fuchsias. I ate my second sandwich on that seat, and made a little drawing on an envelope to fix the scene in my mind, but I don't think I shall ever forget it.

Mabel's sketch of St Pauls on an envelope inserted in the journal.

Then I walked down Ludgate Hill into Fleet Street and turned up on my left into St Bride's Lane. Grandpapa's [8] old office is now a *"Snack Bar"* – a very low looking place. On the left side of the lane rose the gaunt walls of the Church, all the glass gone from the windows. I picked up two little bits that had imbedded themselves in the paving – to take to Mother. The tower is still standing and looks firm and solid; but the bell stands underneath it, still attached to its ropes, with a yawning hole in its shoulder. I noticed the date, 1703 – fifty years after Mary Powell's time [9]. I had meant to go on to the Temple, but I was tired and heart sick and saw no more.

Sunday July 27, 1941

I think the Billeting Officer made a mistake when people realize that once having received evacuees they will never be allowed to get rid of them. I went to ask Dr Morley Davies what success he had had with the committee – and he replied none. They take the view that as Miss Barnes was the last to come into the house she ought to be the first to go. After that I got a certificate from Dr. Johns: Miss Brailsford is not strong enough in health to run her present household without

8 Henry Pooley. The London office of Henry Pooley and Son, 89 Fleet Street.

9 John Milton's Wife.

resident's help. Meantime in spite of his discouraging words, Dr Morley Davies sent me the address of a Mrs Knight in Highland Road, near the Station and today Mrs Lewis has been to see her by appointment. She says she talked to Mrs Knight for an hour and a half and she thinks they will come to an agreement. Once more I have to learn that after my horrible sense of duty has made me keep on a course at very great inconvenience to myself, the sacrifice has been quite unnecessary and those for whom I made it would have been better without – what is the moral of this discovery? One is afraid to press it to a conclusion, for it leads very far – well, in this case – if all goes well, old Mr Lewis will be close to the Station and will go by train to town, saving himself about £1 a week in fares and the danger and discomfort of the blackout. They will have (she says) a large beautiful bedroom with a handsome suite of furniture and a big double bed, instead of the single one they occupy jointly. It is a large five [bed] house in a beautiful garden and oh how welcome they will be to it!

They were away last weekend, for Arthur [10] had 48 hours leave and they all slept in the house at Stamford Hill. He sent me a second of the leaflets [11] dropped by the R.A.F. and this time it was more satisfying – it consisted chiefly of Mr Eden's speech and hints of the new Europe which we hope for. Mother is mending the family socks and shirts for Mrs Wege. They wouldn't accept it without payment so she is taking 6d an hour, to give to the N.C.H.O. [12] – the first money she has earned in her life! Emily Bolam has tried to get them a helper among the Germans and Austrians who foregather at the Meeting House on Sunday afternoons and have a cup of tea – but all in vain. It seems young girls can earn £4 to £5 a week in munitions factories so it is hardly likely they would go into service. Talking of evacuees, there was a painful little scene yesterday at the Library [13], where Mrs Steele and I were helping – Mrs Wylie came in – since her husband is on the Committee and has catalogued the books, she never enters without the air of owning the place and setting everyone to rights – even those who have been officials from the beginning, like Mrs Steele. Mrs Steele had

10 The Lewise's younger son.
11 Propaganda leaflets in German. Mabel was fluent in German.
12 National Children's Home and Orphanage – later called National Children's Home
13 A voluntary library set up by Emily Bolam in the Friends meeting house.

been telling me that 44 books are missing this quarter – mostly borrowed by evacuees who are spurlos verreist [14]. Mrs Wylie chipped in with a loud voice *"Yes, the evacuees are beginning to stink in the nostrils of Amersham."* *"I hope not,"* said a quiet little woman who was standing beside her, obviously one of them. When Mrs Wylie had departed, Mrs Steele went to this stranger and apologized for the rudeness. She told me that the week before there was a similar scene, but worse. Mrs Wylie was again inveighing against the evacuees and again one of their number, a gentlewoman, protested. *"O I don't mean people like you,"* said Mrs Wylie, *"I mean the poor people."* This lady then rebuked her, saying that she hoped she might never know what it was to lose her home and all her belongings: but if she did, she would remember what had passed between them that day. Mrs Wylie is the woman whose voice I heard half-way down Whielden Street proclaiming: *"I may not be clever, but I am intelligent."*

I asked Emily Bolam for news of her evacuee: the young woman whom she took in while she waited to be admitted to Shardeloes to have her baby. She told me a strange tale of this up to date maternity home with its resident woman doctor. The baby was born at four in the morning and at midday the nurses brought the mother a shop meat pie for her dinner. She took a mouthful or two, but refused the rest. Next day the same dinner appeared, and being hungry she ate the whole. She was soon afterwards moved to the sick bay with a very high temperature and covered with spots.

Thursday August 7, 1941

Mr and Mrs Lewis had a shock on Saturday evening. They both walked up by appointment to interview their prospective hostess, Mrs Knight. The husband, a bank manager, was there and he took Mr Lewis apart to consult a timetable and settle what trains he would go in and out of town, and while they were doing that, his wife told Mrs Lewis that she had decided she would rather have a school teacher. I rang up Dr Morley Davies and he will go to see her again, but I don't know what will happen and of course I don't know how far Mrs Lewis is speaking the truth.

14 German: without a trace.

On Sunday I had a visit from Eileen Bowen Davies – a very characteristic one. It was about 5.45pm and I had just begun sunbathing in the back garden, when she came round and stood beside me. I got hurriedly into my frock and she talked to me for some time, lamenting every now and then that she could stay so short a time. She was to catch the next bus to Gerrards Cross, to be in time for supper at home and help her Mother to get it as the maid was out. We waited some time on the road before it dawned upon me that she had missed it by a quarter of an hour. So we came back to wait ¾ of an hour. I said I was sorry I couldn't stay with her as I was alone to get supper for us – and I had to ask her to share our very exiguous meal – and she jumped at it. She said she would like milk to drink and I told her we were short of it. The cheese ration is 2oz per week per head. She began to busy over my music while I went into the kitchen. I soon found there was not time to get supper for three, if she was not to miss another bus – so I laid a tray for her with lettuce and cheese and hot milk and carried it in. So she ate it in a hurry and departed. Both Mrs Pearce and Muriel have warned me of her visits!

On Tuesday came a letter from Arthur to say he had 48 hours embarkation leave – and she [Mrs Lewis] went up by the 8am bus to spend the day with him.

Saturday August 16, 1941

Kind little Dr Morley Davies has found a very desirable home for the Lewises at Westover on Station Road. It is the home of an old lady of 78, Miss Champion, who only occupies three rooms of it. They will be far better off, with a large double bedroom and the dining room to themselves, and he will be able to use the train. I hope they will go next week, only Mr Lewis informed Miss Champion that there was no hurry! Meantime I am sleeping in Miss Bush's bed at the Dawson's. Mr Lewis met me in the hall as I was starting with a heavy suitcase into a black hurricane. He laughed and remarked *"So you're leaving home?"* The gilt is off him I am afraid since he disappeared for twenty minutes in the back garden having stripped the gooseberry bushes of the great berries that I was leaving to ripen. Mother and I had had about four of them! But a couple of weeks ago I bottled 2lbs off other trees, thank goodness.

Monday August 18, 1941

What a queer life! We have had to begin the black-out again, as we went back to ordinary summer time last Sunday week. Every evening darkness comes about five minutes earlier and I, forgetting this, had omitted to draw the curtains in the hall and the kitchen. (We sat late over the 9 o'clock news, for Dorothy Thompson was giving the postscript – a very able, very pro-English American journalist who has been a month in England. The highlight of her talk was a comparison between this little island and Noah's Ark, riding the floods with specimens of every nation of Europe sheltering within her. The papers are full of the meeting on the High Seas between Churchill and Roosevelt and their eight point Atlantic Charter.) Well, when I got up to go to Mrs Dawson's I remembered I had forgotten to have my bath and also to fill the hot bottle I take round, for the weather is very cold and stormy. So I skipped the bath and filled the bottle on the front door step where there was still a faint glimmer of light. Mr Lewis has made me a nice little speech about my kindness to them and his regret that I have to sleep in so many different beds, *"You might be a refugee"*. He hopes we shall go on being friends for ever. I have a chat with the two other evacuees at Willowdene [15] every night when I go in – Miss Holmes, who has been in bed for three weeks with her heart, told me she was evacuated to Amersham with her office and they are working in Copperkins Lane. She has been under Miss Bondfield in some Metropolitan Council. More are also in the house. A young man and his wife, who went away a week ago to have her first baby. He leaves the house at 7.30am to catch the London buss. The last couple of nights as I walked to the house there were two or three searchlights in the dark sky, but we have almost forgotten the sound of our alert. Yet poor little Miss Barnes insists on sleeping with her windows, night sheet, and the heavy curtains drawn across, for fear of having to rise and dress suddenly. She is sleeping badly and waking unrefreshed and I shall be thankful when she moves into the Lewis's room, which has an open chimney. She is the funniest little body – couldn't be called anything but a *"lady"* – yet her clothes must fit impeccably and must be in the latest fashion. I am rather distressed at her goings on in this

15 A neighbouring house where the Dawsons live.

respect, for when we were given coupons for clothes and such things, we were exhorted by the Government to spend as little as possible, but Miss Barnes has been three times to London and fitted herself out with two hats (the first was brown and she had forgotten that all her clothes were blue), a short plaid coat 24/6, and a long summer coat, and a long winter one – three guineas I think – a thick skirt 21/-, a silk frock, a handbag, and she is getting a pair of slippers and an umbrella.

Sunday August 24, 1941

Today marks the closing of a chapter, with the departure of the Lewises. Mr Thompson from the farm 16 came yesterday with his milk cart, to take their luggage and today we were not to see Mrs Lewis again after she left by the 11am bus, to spend the day with Arthur and other relatives, in town. It is the last day of his four days leave. He is waiting now at West Kirby, for a draft to be sent overseas. Poor Mrs Lewis lost all self-control when she heard he was to leave England – jumped at once to the conclusion that he was going to the front somewhere. She said it was a terrible shock, that she was going about in a daze, and that she thought the war made everyone numb. This roused my ire and I remarked it would be a bad lookout for the nation if this were true. Miss Barnes and I both assured her that West Kirby could only be the port for Canada or some such place and certainly not for Egypt or the Far East: but she replied *"I can't be consoled."* Now however he has told her that he is going for further training either to Rhodesia or Canada.

The specialist from London came to see Miss Holmes with a great apparatus of black boxes filled with various electrical appliances. She was immensely relieved by his verdict which I think would have almost crushed any one less keen and plucky. She is to be allowed to go on with her work at the office, seeing that it is here in the quiet country, and not in town. But she is to go for no walks, and to have no excitement of any kind and go to no entertainments. Her breakdown is due first to an operation she had lately: and then to the Blitz – they lived at Hendon and she went daily to and from the office through the ruined streets and worked all day after spending the nights in a shelter

16 Quarrendon Mill Farm. In the valley opposite Mabel's house.

with little or no sleep. Her heart has been weak since childhood.

Miss Barnes is the quaintest little lady and the most unexpected. She was going to have a bath (a great event) and put on her dusting cap, saying to me *"I always cover my head, don't you?"* *"No,"* I said, *"Why do you do it?"* *"Why,"* she explained, *"to save my hair!"* *"What do you want to save it from?"* I asked. *"The water"*, she replied, *"the hard water would turn it grey."*

Sunday September 7, 1941

(It isn't falling that makes one a failure: it's sitting down where you fell – Wayside Pulpit)

We have just had a most happy day with Noel [17]. He sent a wire last Sunday to say he had arrived safe and well – the first we knew of his having left America. He came in a convoy in a Dutch ship and took three weeks. He joined it at New York and sailed alone to Halifax where the convoy was formed in parallel lines, twelve ships in a row, escorted by destroyers. They skirted Iceland in bitter cold weather and had a day among the icebergs. In the North of Ireland the convoy split up and his ship went on to Liverpool. He was distressed at my position with Miss Barnes. I think it is because she suffers so woefully from incontinence of speech that she gets so little done. She will follow me into the bathroom while I brush my teeth or into my bedroom where I am standing in my petticoat – to finish some story about a friend of a friend of hers, whom she has never seen and I have never heard of. It has come to this that I do all the cooking except preparing the veg: and also dust the sitting room. She says nobody could do the housework and the cooking! I ventured to remark that I (and how many other women) had done both for years, in addition to writing books, gardening and looking after Mother. *"Yes,"* she said, *"it's quite different in your own house!"* An illuminating remark. The perpetual drip drip of conversation is most wearing, especially as she insists on getting my opinion and it always differs fundamentally from hers. Noel says his Mrs Pollak [18] is sure to know an educated refugee who would come and do all the work and he is going to try. The last disappointment is

17 Mabel's brother the socialist, writer and broadcaster H.N. Brailsford.

18 His housekeeper.

that I can't go away as Lucy invited me this week, for a few day's rest, as Miss Barnes won't be left alone at night with Mother for fear of air raids. It may be that my kind Miss Bush will help me again – she is coming back tomorrow.

Friday September 12, 1941

This has been a strange week. On Sunday evening Mr Ellis [19] who had been working all week died in his chair. At the same time Mr Glover [20] who had been working all week suddenly became unconscious – he had felt poorly all day.

Sunday September 14, 1941

Mr Glover is out of danger! Two years ago a serum [21] was discovered which can cure any kind of meningitis but one – it also relieves pneumonia at once. But Mr Ellis has gone. I went to see Mrs Ellis the day after the funeral and we talked in the garden, beside the begonias that he had dug up a few hours before his death. She told me that some weeks ago when he was superintending the mending of an outdoor telephone wire a fellow workman fell upon him from a great height, doubling Mr Ellis to the ground but escaping unhurt. He came home that night and said to his wife *"I reckon I saved Tom's life, but it hasn't done me any good."* His death seems to me to lie at Dr. Henderson's door. When the Ellises lived in High Street they kept hens in a garden that paralleled with Dr. Henderson's. One day two men came over the fence, collected his hens and were putting them into crates when Mr Ellis was told and came running up and challenged them. They said they were only doing the Dr's bidding – whereupon Mr Ellis broke open the crates and restored the hens to his own garden and went for the Police Sergeant. He found he was out and already in conference with Dr. Henderson: (so there must be a hole in the ballad at this point, which Laurence's tale does not fill). Mr Ellis poured out his grievance and the sergeant said, *"You know, Dr. that isn't the way to act!"* Whereupon the Dr. offered to shake hands, but Mr. Ellis refused. A fortnight later, Dr Henderson was most unfortunately elected to be

19 Lives at Elmcroft.
20 Lives next door to Mabel at Martindale.
21 Antibiotics.

Panel doctor for the Post Office employees: But the feud went on both sides. Mr Ellis was very ill with colic: but the Dr. looked at him from afar and pronounced it lumbago. That night he passed blood and the Dr., without going up to see him, told Mrs Ellis he was suffering from gallstones and he would get him admitted to a hospital.
I remember this very well, for we were at Little Elms. The hospital found no trace of gallstones, but treated him for his stomach and he came back well. Ever since, Mr. Ellis has tried not to report any illness. He would have reported the injury of the big man falling on him, and he so tiny, if there had been any other Dr. – for ever since he has been having attacks of numbness in different parts of the body and Lawrence thinks a clot of blood had formed which went at last to his heart. Mrs Ellis was making him a cup of tea and brought it to feed him, as she thought with his hand hanging down, playing with the dog. When she saw his face, she rushed to the telephone and begged the Dr. twice to come as her husband had collapsed and she thought he had gone. He said twice, *"No I can't come. It is too far."* and finally, *"You had better get Dr. Green."* He signed a death certificate for heart failure following long standing heart trouble – he had not seen him for two years.

Sunday September 21, 1941

Mr Glover died of pneumonia the day after he had been pronounced out of danger. Mr. Stubbings took his wife to Aylesbury early in the morning and she stayed there till 5.10pm when he died, without regaining consciousness. Mrs Stubbings came to tell me after tea, and ask if I knew the address of her Mother or Sister so that we could telephone to them but I don't. Marjorie, as I now call her, seems so utterly alone. She herself however summoned two Glover cousins to Aylesbury and they with Mr Stubbings made all arrangements. The funeral was on Friday – driving from Aylesbury to the Church, where we met it. After a short service in the Church [22] there was a long walk behind the coffin, through the Church grounds and over the bridge, through the old Church Yard and right through the new, which was as it always is, beautiful with flowers and bright green. It was pitiful to see

22 St Mary's, Amersham.

From the Church grounds over the little bridge and through the old Church Yard.

Marjorie walk alone, most erect and grasping my bunch of red roses. She was followed, not accompanied, by the two cousins: then came Mrs Stubbings and I and then some score of men from Mr Glover's works. I suppose it was a case of rigid etiquette and precedence, but I could gladly have defied it: and when we grouped ourselves round the grave I did step forward and take her arm. At the end the Rector turned away and walked back to the Church without a word of sympathy. Marjorie flung the roses into the open grave and hurried away. Her Mother came on Thursday evening, travelling from near Woolacombe, where she was on holiday. Next day the boys began school at Berkhamsted Grammar School. Margaret Green [23] has been given notice at her lodgings and the natural thing would be for her to come back to Martindale – if she were not Margaret Green, Marjorie told her some time ago that there was only one person she ought to live with and that was herself.

I have arranged for Miss Barnes to stay on. She is doing very differently now and seems anxious to help me and to be kind. I am a little dubious of how things will go when we have the three fires!! But it is a relief not to have to change. We had a long visit from the Lewises after tea yesterday. Their son, Arthur, is still at West Kirby, doing nothing but wash dishes and prepare vegetables. All the men who went there with him have been sent weeks ago to Canada and South Africa to finish their training. He has had three leaves already, when his Mother has met him in London and he slept at his brother's house.

23 Thought to be Marjorie's mother.

Tuesday September 30, 1941

Last Friday I had a delightful day in London with Noel. It all arose from his visit the other day. I told Miss Barnes he was distressed that I had no time for writing and she very cheerfully assured me that it could be arranged and I am to have from 9 – 11am every morning. The following Sunday I was in the little Chapel [24] (for Mr Hill had come to ask me to begin playing again in the mornings) and the beauty and dramatic force of one of Charles Wesley's hymns struck at my heart as George Fox would say. I had not been in Church for more than a year! At the same moment I was filled with the desire to write his life and that is what I am now beginning. I hope it was a true inspiration – it was the last thing I expected and certainly came to me from outside: Well, Noel asked me to invite myself to Town and I went to the flat [25] last Friday. I felt very sad to see all the traces of Clare's [26] occupation. Noel had found many of her old oil paintings when he cleared out the attic – chiefly done on holiday in France. I took him produce from the garden: glorious roses, a bunch of onions - worth their weight in gold, three preserved eggs, ditto, and three cobs of Indian corn which I have grown very successfully and prolifically from 6d of seed, in the patch of garden prepared by the goats and hens! We tried to get lunch opposite the Belsize Park Station, in the same shop where we took our last meal with Clare the day before she sailed, but nothing was ready at twelve and we went straight to the National Gallery, to take our seats for the one o'clock Concert. We found two long counters of coffee, tea, and sandwiches, served by fashionable ladies and doing a roaring trade, but just as we went in we met Muriel Juniper whom I had known as a shock-headed Backfisch [27] about fifteen years ago, when she used to come to help Clare with her printing. I didn't recognise her – so much was she changed and sobered and saddened. Noel asked her to come to the flat and choose anything of Clare's that would not keep and that she would make use

Amersham Methodist Church,
Old Amersham.

24 Methodist chapel, Amersham High Street.
25 Noel's flat: 37 Belsize Park Gardens NW3, now has a blue plaque in his name.
26 Clare Leighton, artist, writer and engraver. Moved to the USA in 1938.
27 German: teenage girl.

of. Meanwhile I took our tickets – all are 1/-. We got sandwiches and coffee and sat down on the steps to eat them with most of the people who were going to the Concert. It was a delightful audience of music lovers, delightful to play to, I think. There was a trio – piano, Millicent Silver, who seemed to me a faultless player, both delicate and strong – flute, a young man, and oboe, a young girl, Joy Boughton, who played some of her (no doubt) Father's music [28] for a solo. When we came out we turned into part of the building which was given up to the War Artists' Exhibition. The only beautiful things were two very large drawings of Muirhead Bone's [29] – a view of St Pauls from a roof near the burnt out St Bride's Church; and a picture of an aircraft carrier – each looked the work of a lifetime. The pictures of air raid shelters were truly ghastly – bringing a strange sense of shame to the beholder. The National Gallery has barely escaped destruction, yet seems quite unhurt. The Government building on its left is quite bombed out. We walked then to St. James' Square, seeing very little sign of damage, but one large house at the far corner has been obliterated. Some windows of the Library [30] have been smashed and a notice warns readers to be careful of *"glass in books"*?

Saturday October 11, 1941

Yesterday we had poor old Mrs Glover to tea. [31] She reminds me of Naomi. [32] She has lost, since we know her – in ten years – husband and home, son, two daughters and a son-in-law. She is living at Mrs Barrett's (a cottage, as she says, and very different from what she has been accustomed to), but she has many of her own things about her in the little sitting room and Mrs Barrett is as good to her as a daughter. But Mrs Barrett has little time to devote to her – she has an evacuee schoolboy. At the weekends his parents come down and the three of them sleep in the little room at the back (a proceeding much deprecated by all who know of it!). She has no Ruth [33] for her daughter-in-law, though Marjorie has been very kind and attentive

28 Rutland Boughton 1878 – 1960.
29 Sir Muirhead Bone 1876 – 1953, war artist. Friend of Mabel and Noel.
30 The London Library.
31 Marjorie Glover's Mother-in-Law.
32 Biblical reference from the Old Testament: The Book of Ruth
33 Biblical reference. Daughter-in-law of Naomi.

since these troubles came upon them both. As she was leaving, I rang up Marjorie to see if it would be convenient for Mrs Glover to call. She begged, quite nicely, to be excused. She was putting the children to bed, she said (hardly at 5.45pm) and then had Jill to milk before the blackout. Michael was away from school with asthma, the second attack in three weeks and she herself feels very unwell, not being able to sleep. I wish she would go back to office work which she likes and send the boys to boarding school where they would have some discipline and training. She has not yet returned Mother's stockings which we lent her for the funeral. She says they are lost! And Miss Isaacs has not yet got back her very pretty hat (or had not last time I heard).

Such is life in this corner of Bucks: While Russia is facing the crisis of her struggle and every English newspaper is full of indignant protests at the little we are doing to help her.

Monday October 20, 1941

Is snobbery become the prerogative of the lower middle classes (and of course of the Church)? I have been meditating on Miss Barnes insistence that she is a lady. She refused a good place before coming to us, because she would have had to have her meals alone – a thing I think that a real gentlewoman would insist upon. But the remark that really shocked me came after her visit to the little Wesleyan Chapel. She said the singing was good and she had enjoyed it, though it wasn't what she had been used to in town, *"Of course they are poor people's voices"*. Probably she only meant they were untrained.

We have had Army Manoeuvres here, lasting for a week and involving the whole of the Southern Command. Here on the London Road we saw and heard little, except for one night, when heavy lorries, tanks and motor cycles were passing from dusk to dawn. I think the Generals are having hard work to keep the Army happy and employed: they are itching to get across the Channel and remove some of the pressure on the Russians. I suspect this is the reason behind the present publication of Gort's [34] despatches, leading up to Dunkirk, which show the impossibility of facing up to the Germans without an

34 6th Viscount Gort (1886–1946).

overwhelming supply of munitions. Yesterday in London there was a meeting of half a million shop stewards and munition workers, [35] to urge upon the Goverment the formulation of a second front, and pledging themselves to keep it adequately supplied.

Whilst this forms our background, and so far a distant one, Dr. Ticciati [36] is giving a new series of lectures on Friday afternoons, dealing chiefly with composition: Unity of Subject and of mood. He began with an example of half a dozen of the most beautiful melodies strung together – illustrating lack of unity – saying in passing apropos unity of mood – a listener cannot be expected to change in five minutes from ecstasy to despair. To illustrate unity of subject he played the overture to the Rheingold, written of nothing but one common chord - G major, I think – representing the beginning of creation. He played also Brahms' 24 variations on a theme of Handel's. I should have enjoyed them better if there had been only six – my fault of course. I spend the morning in a violent gale providing him and Mrs Pearce with a large electric fire and a small blackboard and easel.

35 Believed to mean representatives of half a million workers.

36 Pianist and composer at the Music Studio, Chestnut Close, Amersham.

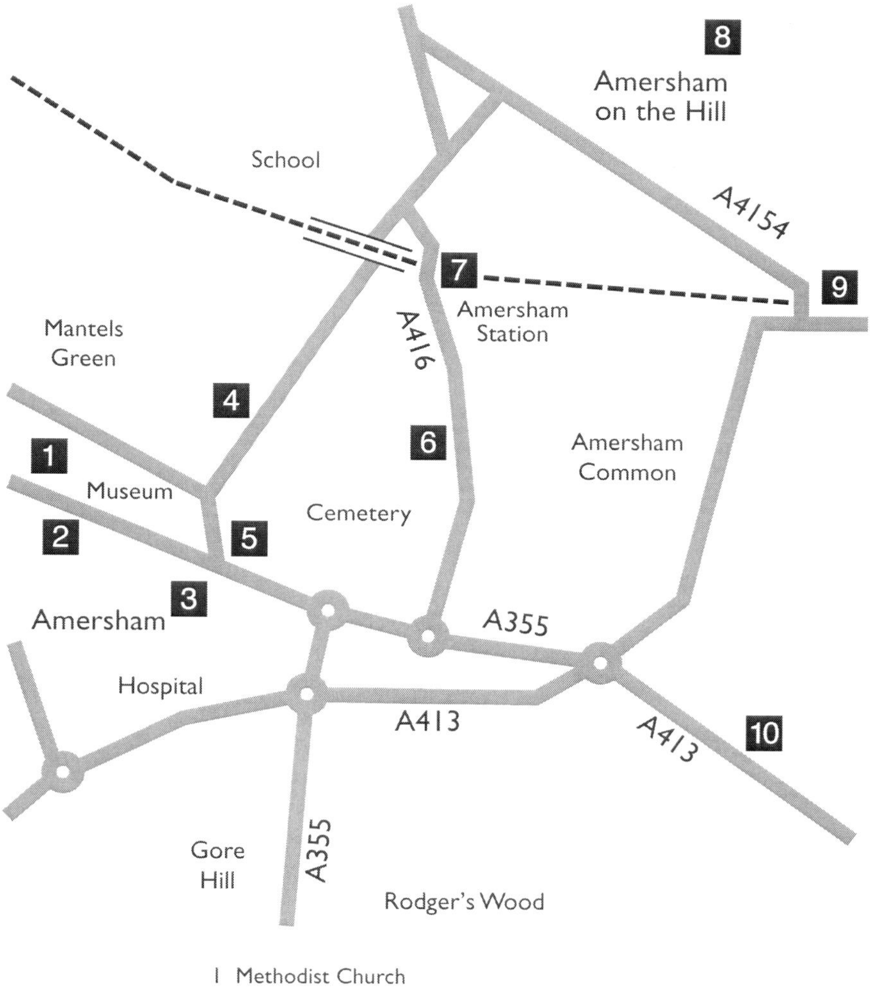

1 Methodist Church
2 High Street
3 Friends Meeting House
4 Rectory Hill
5 St.Mary's Church were Mr Glover is buried
6 Station Road
7 Amersham Station
8 Music Studio
9 Black Horse Bridge
10 Mabel's House, Greylands

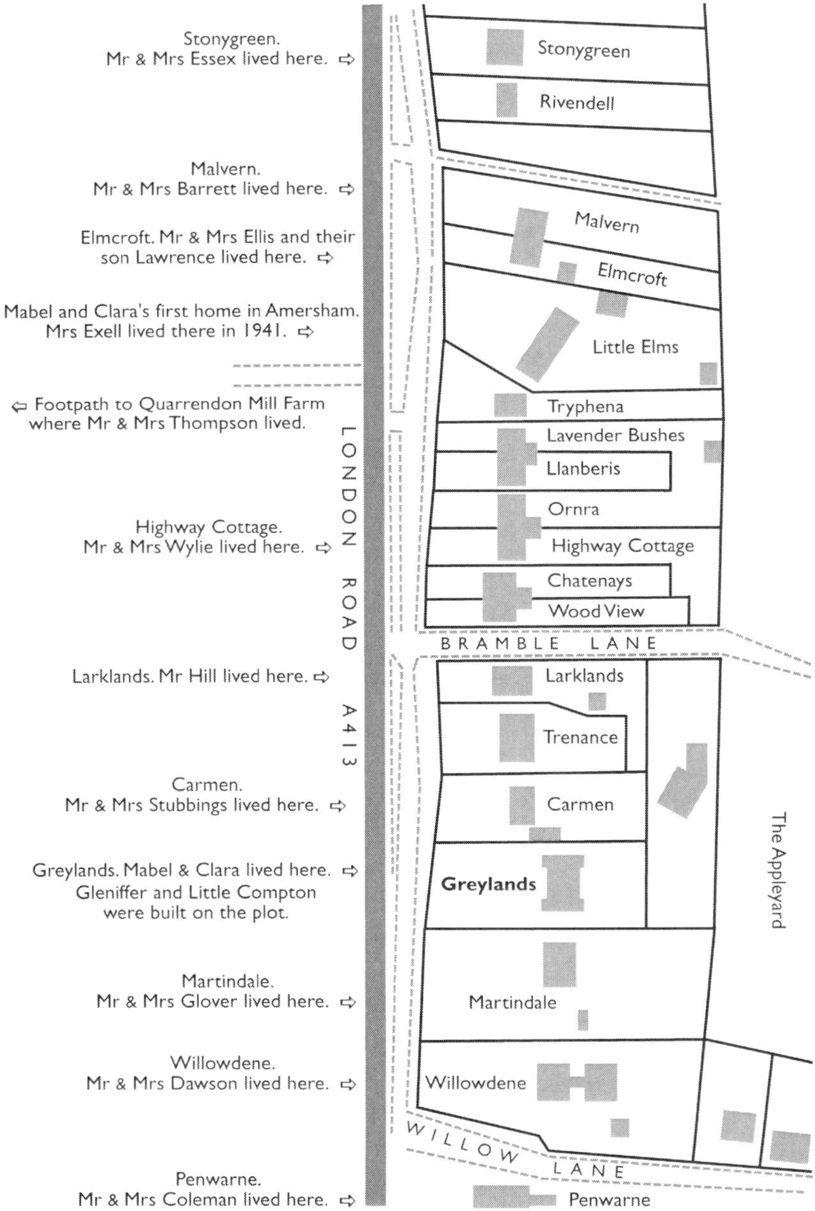
Stonygreen.
Mr & Mrs Essex lived here.
Malvern.
Mr & Mrs Barrett lived here.
Elmcroft. Mr & Mrs Ellis and their son Lawrence lived here.
Mabel and Clara's first home in Amersham. Mrs Exell lived there in 1941.
Footpath to Quarrendon Mill Farm where Mr & Mrs Thompson lived.
Highway Cottage.
Mr & Mrs Wylie lived here.
Larklands. Mr Hill lived here.
Carmen.
Mr & Mrs Stubbings lived here.
Greylands. Mabel & Clara lived here.
Gleniffer and Little Compton were built on the plot.
Martindale.
Mr & Mrs Glover lived here.
Willowdene.
Mr & Mrs Dawson lived here.
Penwarne.
Mr & Mrs Coleman lived here.
LONDON ROAD A413
Stonygreen
Rivendell
Malvern
Elmcroft
Little Elms
Tryphena
Lavender Bushes
Llanberis
Ornra
Highway Cottage
Chatenays
Wood View
BRAMBLE LANE
Larklands
Trenance
Carmen
Greylands
Martindale
Willowdene
The Appleyard
WILLOW LANE
Penwarne

1942

Monday March 9, 1942

I thought this new volume [37] would have been about the War. Never before have we been depressed as we were through January and February – certainly not at the time of Dunkirk – our first defeat which was more than half a victory. But as the Pacific bases fell one by one to the Japs, after we had been assured one by one that our positions were impregnable and we were withdrawing according to plan – and even in Libya the same hoary form of words was used to camouflage failure. I think everyone felt as I did that all the slaughter and suffering and toil in the factories was a useless waste and that any news of defence would be immediately followed by news of retreat. It was in the midst of this that Dr. Ticciati began his course of musical talks on Beethoven and changed the whole world for me. Last week, the third, was the finest of all. He played the Waldstein and the Appassionata and never in my life at any concert have I heard such playing. It was to me like an illumination and a baptism or to put it more prosaically, like a holiday at the seaside, for which I ceased to hanker. Mrs Pearce was ill – she was present but could only crouch in front of the fire. She asked me to help him with the tea and to pour out when we had made it. There were only present, besides Eileen Bowen-Davies and the lovely old lady *"Violet Defries"*, who is on the most delightful terms with Dr Ticciati. I think she must have taught him to speak his excellent English, for she was teasing him about it. She is a Jewess, though she doesn't look it and she was talking about the beauty of the Psalms (strange that Adelaide [38] should have mentioned them in her letter that same day with reference to the Spring.) *"Violet"* quoted the exhortation *"Commence with thine own heart upon thy bed, and be still"* – only she altered it to silent which seemed to me to hurt it both in sense and rhythm. Eileen B.D. seemed much softened and very expansive. She apologised for talking so much saying that in her own home no one paid any attention to what she said or thought, so it was a temptation to talk too much when she found herself in sympathetic company. There had been a large assembly – mostly I think Jews. A fat old couple, most appreciative, who sat in front of me are called Nathan.

37 This was the first entry in a new exercise book.
38 Relative of Mabel's.

Another newcomer is a very handsome loud looking Portuguese Jewess called Mrs Cavalho. She is immensely rich and brings a carnation each week which she fastens in Dr. Ticciati's buttonhole. She and the equally loud and admiring Mrs West provide a great element of comedy and are mutually antagonistic. The week before last, Mrs Cavalho had been going to stay to tea but excused herself at the last minute. She wrote afterwards to Dr Ticciati that she couldn't stay with that *"yellow-haired woman"* – a very mild description of one whose hair is the most fiery red! I arranged to come next day and get Mrs Pearce her tea, as that is the day he is playing the organ at the synagogue. [39] She was lying ill with shingles, in the music room – very untidy and undusted for the woman had not come at all and sent her little girl of 14. We had a very long and very happy talk about the Wesleys. She is greatly interested, as her grandfather was a Wesleyan Minister named Hoby, and built the London Great Queen Street Chapel. When it came on the market, her cousin bought it and turned it, I think she said, into a Cinema.

Yesterday we had Dr Ticciati to dinner. It was a joy to me and the food was a success. He neither smokes nor drinks and Mrs Pearce has turned him into an ardent vegetarian. He horrified me by the news that he is due to be called up in September (at the age of 45 I suppose – no he will be 49) and would no doubt be sent to work on the land. He has applied for an engagement as lecturer to the troops and has had a very encouraging reply, asking him to go up for an interview on Thursday. He would give lectures in the style of what he has given us, beginning with *"How to listen to Music"*. He is going to give the Sermon on a future Sunday at the Synagogue (surely a very broad minded place) on *"A Musician looks at Religion"*. He took back in his music case a large basin of Benger's Food [40] for Mrs Pearce and some dropped scones for their tea. Today he will be out giving a lesson at Great Missenden, so I am going again to get Mrs Pearce her tea.

On Friday morning we had a hurried visit from Min Green. She seems to be continually beset with contretemps. She had just had word from the men who were moving her new caravan, that it has stuck fast in the deep mud beside a gate and cannot be moved till the ground

39 West London Synagogue, near Marble Arch.
40 A drink for invalids similar to dried milk and enriched with vitamins.

dries. I suggested sacking or planks in front of the wheels. Furthermore, when she wished to get out some money to pay for this caravan, she heard that her property had been put in the hands of the Public Trustee for foreign funds (I forget his correct title) on the mistaken idea that she was still at Greifswald. That Thursday night I had been kept awake till 12.30am by the blazing light in Mrs Glover's kitchen. I was really frightened, for if any enemy plane had been about, it would surely have proved an irresistible target. So I went to find out when the young Warden would be at home, determined at long last to put him on her track. By great good luck, Miss Isaacs was expecting Mr Goulter the chief Warden to call at Willowdene that morning and put the matter before him, from her own knowledge. I don't know what happened but I haven't seen a streak of light since. Alas this was a delusion and once again the view from my bedroom reminds one of the conflict in Excelsior *"In cottage homes he saw the light of household fires gleam"* [41]

Wednesday March 25, 1942

I had the most crackbrained and the most interesting dream last night. I was talking a week or two ago at Mrs Pearce's to an oldish gentleman, Mr Milburn, a great admirer of Noel's, who is an authority on Indian Scriptures. He is to give a talk at the Studio on his ideas of how religion should help to build the new world after the War.

I dreamed last night that I was at a meeting to discuss this and the speaker said: The New World must be built by manual labour. But someone in the audience got up and said (adapting a lovely childs' poem that I have not read for years!) *"You spell it with an E, an E, an E for unless we have Emanuel, God, with us all our labour will not build a New World."* They labour in vain that build it.

Thursday March 26, 1942

I have not been to Mrs Pearce since Tuesday. That was a very happy visit. She had moved into her original front bedroom, now Dr. Ticciati's, while he took her pupils in the music room. In the afternoon he was expecting one of his own – a medical Dr. Robinson – and had

41 Longfellow.

got ready two trays for them and us and bought a plateful of little jam tarts! I took them a dozen griddle scones and some cream cheese. We could hear the lesson being given – the man can play extremely well, but part of the time was given to five finger exercises. Mrs Bunney came in for a minute bringing one egg – the rationed amount from Sainsbury's. She is the wife of the Socialist Mr Bunney, who tried for the Town Council a few years ago. He is so much a Socialist that he sends his delightful little girl of nine to the Council School, where, being very bright, she only uses half her brain, assimilates all sorts of bad words, and takes heed to no sort of correction gentler than the rod. [42] This same Mr Bunney, socialist as he is must be a real Turk in his marriage relations. Mrs Pearce asked Mrs Bunney who was going to the Station, to give a note for her to Dr Ticciati, who was arriving at the same time. She explained that she couldn't take it, as her husband wouldn't like it – he couldn't bear her to speak to a man in that way! She looks almost a girl, with a sweet good face.

Friday April 3, 1942 – Good Friday

I want to tell you about Dr. Ticciati's adventures yesterday. I wasn't expecting to see him this morning, nor was Mrs Pearce. He had been in London all day and you know I gave Mrs Pearce her supper and she settled down and had a very good night. She had arranged with the child of fourteen to come at 8am and give her her breakfast, but when the child saw that Dr. Ticciati had come back, she went straight home, leaving the kitchen a terrible pigsty. I heard him practicing as soon as I walked up the path and Mrs Pearce sent me in to listen while she got dressed – she had just lain quiet till I arrived. They want me to call them by their Christian names, which I take as a very great compliment, but I don't find it very easy with *"Georgia"*. But I must because she seemed so grateful and relieved when I did. She says it is once in a blue moon that she asks a friend to do it and she is superstitious about it, for if they don't something always occurs to break the friendship. *"Francesco"* didn't play but talked, telling me his adventures of yesterday. First he went by appointment to interview the head of the Education Board for the Troops and had a very

42 This is unsubstantiated gossip. The Bunneys were members of the Society of Friends and all four of their children went to Quaker boarding schools.

encouraging reception. There is no vacancy for a lecturer at the moment, but a new Director has just been appointed who intends to enlarge the scope of the lectures and to lay special stress on music and then he would be sure of an engagement very soon.

From there he went, also by appointment, to see a Mrs Van der Elst.[43] I know her name very well from seeing various reports in the paper from time to time, of collisions she has had with the authorities. She is a strong opponent of capital punishment, and when an execution was to take place, she drove up under the walls of the prison and gathered a crowd round her, shouting and distributing pamphlets. The other time was in connection with a portrait she had commissioned some artist to paint for her, and refused to pay for, as she considered it unflattering. I remember she represented herself as a judge of art. She is an immensely wealthy woman: her husband made a fortune with Shavex shaving cream, [44] and since his death she is managing it with great ability, particularly in the line of advertisements. Well the first Francesco heard of her was from a music publisher. It seems she fancies herself as a composer, but knowing nothing about music, she has to get some very competent artist to take down the notes as they fall from her lips and then take them home and harmonize them. She calls them her Symphonies. She lies back in her Armchair with her eyes shut and croons forth about six notes. Halfway through the evening she will say *"I shall begin to be inspired about 9 o'clock, so will you go now and have supper somewhere(!) and come back in an hour and we will work till 2am in the morning and you can spend the night here."* I don't know how he escaped last night but he got home about 10.30pm and crept about in the dark trying not to wake Mrs Pearce, and knocks down the whole rack of plates in the kitchen. He is to get £10 for each séance and the working up of her melodies will take him about six hours. She will then pay the music publisher to publish them under her name. [45] This is called *"ghosting"*. I know it is often done in the book world. It seems to me a shady proceeding and I said so. He agreed and said he had tried to get out of it by putting up his

43 Mrs Violet Van der Elst (1882–1966), millionairess, anti-capital punishment campaigner, eccentric.

44 In fact her husband was an artist, and it was Violet who made the fortune with Shavex – before her marriage.

45 Mabel notes: *"£2 a sheet. The publisher calls it aspidistra music"*.

fees, and at any rate he says she will soon get tired of him and tell him he does not understand the quality of her inspirations. He says she lives in an unbelievably rich and hideous house and has no friends, for she suspects every one of designs on her money.

Mrs Pearce told me how she came to know Dr. Robinson, who has taken her to his home this morning. It was when she lived in Amersham. She was terribly poor and had only 10/- in the house, which had to go to pay the daily woman. But she was due to go to Manchester, where she still gives lessons, and had nothing to pay her fare. She could think of no expedient but going by way of London and borrowing from her son-in-law, but she hated to do that, and decided to pray about it. In the course of the afternoon the telephone bell rang and a young man asked if he might come over and have a lesson. It was Dr. Robinson and he had a lesson at 7pm that evening. He enjoyed it so much that he said he would take the course of six lessons and before he left he paid £3/3s in advance! Much more than the fare to Manchester.

There is a literary-philosophical-religious meeting at the Studio on the last Sunday of every month. (I did the little poster for the last one, as Mrs Pearce was ill). She said she and Dr. Ticciati wanted to ask Noel for one, but felt it was too small an occasion for him, but did I think he would give them a talk some day when he was with us. I looked up dates and found that your [46] coming birthday was on the last Saturday in June, so in my last letter to Noel I asked him to come to us for the weekend and we would both go to the Studio on the next day. They say that the discussions following are generally the best part, and I think most of the members are students of Noel's work.

The domestic situation is quite desperate for some families, now that all able bodied women have been called up for Munitions. The worst case I know is of the Sloley's – an old Father of 95 who can't be left alone lest he should came to harm – and a devoted bachelor son of 61 who has just retired from some important job in town. They live in a big house in Amersham on the Hill and were looked after by a working housekeeper. She has left them and they can't even find a woman for two hours to scrub the floors.

46 Her Mother's.

The other is the lady who keeps the *"Daisy Shop"*, a beautiful little shop that sells fine china and such things near the P.O. I heard from Millicent that she was a friend of the Muirhead Bones. I called therefore on Friday morning, partly to make friends, partly to buy a very lovely Easter card for Miss Barnes to send to a friend, and partly to ask her to exhibit a little poster of Dr. Ticciati's next Concert, which is to be next Sunday at the Tory Uncle's Studio in support of the *"Aid to Russia"*. We did make friends; she has stayed several times with Muirhead and Gertrude when the boys were boys (but I don't know her name!). She told me she has had no help of any kind in house or shop for the whole of the winter and gets so tired that she feels sometimes she must give it up. It isn't just like keeping your house going, for the shop bell will ring just when she is boiling the milk or at the top of the house making a bed. She has a big West Highland, very like Susan. [47]

Sunday April 19, 1942

These past weeks have been rather heady wine for me – after the long cold dark winter. When Mother was stone deaf and my intercourse with my fellow beings confined almost exclusively to the society of Miss Barnes, Charles Wesley it was who kept the spark of intellect alive in me! But since the middle of March I seem to have been taken inside the home of two people who give me all I have ever asked for or needed in the way of companionship. This is the third time since we came to Amersham that I have tried to play good Samaritan to neighbours who were ill and in sore need. The first was from Little Elms [48]– when all the Bolam's, including Godfrey, who was then a new baby, were down with flu and pneumonia. I gained from that fortnight the love and friendship of Emily Bolam and an admiration for her that has gone on growing in the thirteen (I think) years that are past. Then about three years ago, came the Thompsons at the Quarrendon Farm opposite – all the family again down with 'flu and unable for some days to find any help but mine – together with visits from the District Nurse and Lawrence Ellis, both of whom I enlisted. There too, though we

47 Mabel's dog.
48 A smaller house not far from Greylands to which they moved in 1923 after her Father died.

seldom meet, I feel I made a true friend in Mrs Thompson. But I have never had anything like the past three weeks, when every day Mrs Pearce, Dr. Ticciati and I have talked more freely and found more subjects in common, and besides, while I have made tea and acted as *"receptionist"* to an orchestra that uses the Music Room for practice, I have got to know other delightful people – chiefly the Blacks – whom I met at tea the first time Mrs Pearce asked me to meet Dr. Ticciati 18 months ago. She has got a job at Chesham teaching history, her favourite subject, in an evacuated school. He is working hard for Russian friends. Then a young Mrs Nathan – a German Jewess and a member of the orchestra, who holds a degree in Economics – and a Mrs Lilienfeld, an Austrian Jewess from Vienna, who has a glorious voice. These two last had tea one day last week and Mrs Black turned up before it was finished, bringing a big rice pudding for supper and some tarts. Mrs Lilienfeld is giving lessons in German to the troops stationed at Great Missenden. An officer came to take her there in his car, but they had scarcely started before they were stopped and her papers demanded – apparently the police thought she was joy riding and wasting petrol. So now she has offered to go by bus! She is coming to have tea with us in a few days, after I am not so tied with Mrs Pearce. She lives near Millicent, she and her husband, as evacuees from town .... I have continued to get up at 6.30am though I no longer have two fires to do before breakfast and all this mental springtime has had for background a glory of sunshine and golden daffodils. There is so much to do in the garden that practising [49] is crowded out unless I take the time before breakfast. Friday crowded everything I most love into itself – music first; cooking the dinner; dusting Mother's room; an hour at Charles Wesley; and an hour at gardening. Then a rest and bicycle up the hill to the Music Studio – Francesco has got tea already, as I had not known whether I would have my bicycle to ride. The evening before, I had leaned it against the wall near the front door, where Mrs Black and I were sitting as she said, to ripen like peaches, and I saw the back tyre deflating itself under the hot sun. There is a big patch on the inner tube which had come loose for the second time. However Laurence came in the morning and mended it again for me.

49 Assumed to be a reference to the piano.

We settled Mrs Pearce with cushions and a footstool and sat at the front door for tea. Meanwhile I washed up. Francesco finished typing his sermon. I had heard it once and had made a mental note of some emendations, but the Blacks had turned up before I could speak of them. So now he gave me the Ms. in my own hand – He writes a clear and extraordinarily vivid style – with every now and then some slight nuance upon a word, such as no Englishman would use, which gives it back the richness of its original meaning. I think he feels to the English language as a person would feel to the Bible, who had not been brought up on it. It was a great joy to me to be able to help him, for it seemed like paying back in my own coin a little of what he has given me in his speaking of the way that the accepted truths of age become the myths of the next (these are not his words) he mentioned Galen's treatment of wounds by cauterisation followed by immersion in boiling oil. It was not till the 16th Century that Ambroise Paré discovered a simple bandage would do the job better. I could give Francesco, of course, my favourite quotation from Cromwell *"I beseech you by the mercies of Christ, think it possible you may be mistaken"* and also *"Beauty is Truth. Truth Beauty."* which he had not quoted quite correctly.

Alas Mrs Pearce was forbidden by the doctor to go to the Synagogue on Saturday. I went at 12pm and got dinner for her and me in the back garden, and put her to rest there while I washed up and mended Francesco's socks! Then finding that she had had to put off her going to London till after the meeting of the Orchestra, we arranged that she should get off by the 5.40pm train and I came back after seeing her off, to shut up the house when the membership departed. The Concert was at 3pm on Sunday in the Rudolf Steiner Hall, and made about £50 for sick relief.

Saturday May 2, 1942

I have just come back from Mrs Crawshaw's funeral – my first Quaker burying. Any ceremony could not fail to be beautiful and moving in such a setting. The graveyard lies between the Jordans Meeting House and the Hostel, a little to the west of the land where William Penn and Guli are buried. You walk to it, if you will, through the Hostel Garden,

now glowing with wall flowers and past the sunk garden where the roses will soon be in bloom. Then through the cherry orchard of old trees, decked to the topmost bough with white blossom. It faces a hillside, sparsely covered with young beech trees just bursting into leaf, and from somewhere on the fresh green of the grass came the cry of a new-born lamb. People were already gathering in the little enclosure – it is a truly democratic resting place, for all the gravestones are of one size and pattern like the simple upright lozenge that marks the grave of William Penn and all the inscriptions confined to statements of name, birth, and death. Everything in the ceremony appealed to me – except the omission of any word from the Bible – but even that was supplied for me by the little cripple with whom I was standing – Dora Larg – who had been for over twenty years a worker at Friends House, on the Social Service Council, where I used to see her. She told me, and there was evidently a whole story behind it – that she had resigned when Friends House [50] was evacuated to Jordans after the Blitz. She said, and I utterly agreed with her, that she didn't judge anyone else, but for her part she felt that they of all people ought to have stayed at the post of danger.

When we turned away from the grave she said *"How could we be sad on such a day"*, meaning, I think, that we must feel at unity with the creation where all around us men were putting bare grain into the

50 Euston Road, London, NW1.

earth to be raised a glorious body. When they placed the coffin on the trestles, we stood in silence for about five minutes. Then some man friend made a rather trite speech followed by the reading of *"Crossing the Bar"* by Mr. Nicholson, Clerk to the Society of Friends, whom I used to know in London. [51] An Announcement followed, that a meeting (Memorial) would be held at the Meeting House, at which it was hoped we would all be present and that was all. We filed off slowly over the grass and into the Meeting House, where the door stood wide open to the sun and the song of the birds. Again there was a long period of silence, but Ethel Morland looked round and saw me and I was greatly rewarded by the delighted smile on her sad face. Only two Friends were moved to speak, and both spoke very simply and movingly about Mrs Crawshaw's influence in Jordans – her love and sympathy with the young people, her kindness in welcoming newcomers and introducing them to the others, and her sense of humour which often came to the rescue in smoothing over awkward situations. There was one prayer, at which we all stood and the meeting ended with an invitation to all Friends from a distance to stay for tea at Jordans Hostel. This was arranged by Mrs Crawshaw's express desire before her death.

I sat between Ethel and Mr Stanley Forward. I knew him also at Friends House, but couldn't put a name to him – indeed it was great fun to meet one and another who knew that they knew me, but not who I was, and then to feel their warm welcome when they learned it again. Ethel told a non-Friend at our table that she must not be shocked to see them so happy – and added in the identical words of Charles Wesley about the early Methodists – that funerals were amongst the most joyous events in the Society of Friends. I got to Jordans early and called on Nance Beakbane – to find her lying ill on the sofa having just arrived from a nursing home. She has had two bad heart attacks, and there was no one then to look after her in the house.

This week we had Mrs Pearce to spend Tuesday night with us and most of the day before and after. It was a very happy time and I learned to know and admire her even more than I did. She has had a very hard struggle ever since her marriage, for her husband turned out to be a

51 Tennyson, Crossing the Bar. A poem.

consumptive bordering at times on insanity. He had an excellent livelihood (I think as a solicitor) when he could attend to it, but she had to earn money to keep the home together and educate the child Stella. She was very delicate too and had, I think five or six miscarriages before the living child was born. She did a good deal of journalism in addition to music writing regularly for Robert Blatchford [52] at the Clarion. He is still an intimate friend and is over ninety. Francesco was to have come for Georgia in the morning and spend the day with us, but Mrs Cavalho altered the time of her lesson and elected to have it that evening, so it was not till the 7.20pm bus that he arrived. We were teasing Mother who began asking at tea time when will Dr Ticciati be here? Georgia asked her if she couldn't wait two hours for him? It was getting a little chilly then, so we all packed into the glass part of the verandah – Mother on her couch and Georgia on the garden stretcher beside her – Francesco at Mothers feet and I facing him at Georgia's. It was such a short time, for in war conditions the last bus that passes here for Amersham on the Hill is at 8.30pm. I wanted to take Francesco round the garden to see the fruit trees in bloom but before we started he asked Mother to go into the sitting room, so that he could play for her. And when we came back, via the Kitchen, she was waiting for him on the sofa beside the piano. She wrote next day to tell Noel how he asked to play for her and has talked of it ever since.

For the past six weeks Francesco has been troubled with pain in his right arm, and at last made up his mind to consult my Dr. Cipriax – a very suitable man to go to, for he told me that a larger part of his clientele were artistes from the Queens Hall who needed to be patched up before fulfilling their engagement. (Clare had sent me to him and it was he who asked me if it was my brother who is *"Mr. Clare Leighton"*? for which I have never quite forgiven all concerned). Francesco rang me up yesterday morning. Dr Cipriax found a thickening of the muscle due to excessive practising and has forbidden him to practise, though he may play the organ on Saturday and Sunday. He is to go for treatment three times a week, and sounded terribly anxious about the expense. Nothing at all had been said about it at this first interview and he didn't know whether Dr Cipriax would expect him to be able to pay

52 Robert Peel Glanville Blatchford (17 March 1851 – 17 December 1943). See appendix.

large fees. I saw that I would have to confess and I hoped he would not mind, but I had sent another letter to the Dr. to tell him that Francesco was in low water (I forget how I put it) owing to war conditions. He exclaimed *"Did you do that? O what a relief: then it will be all right"*. This is the man who has just made £50 for Relief work in Greece in the space of an hour and a half: and has refused a retaining fee of £800 a year from the BBC that he may have time for composition.

I must set down another curious story. Georgia told me of an answer to her prayer. Her husband had had a very bad attack (of melancholia I think) and had had to be put away for some time. Then she got him out, and took him away at once, with little Stella, to the seaside. They were all sitting by the sea shore, and he undressed to go in to bathe. He turned back and took the engagement ring she had given him off his finger (a broad plain band that she always wears now above her wedding ring) asking her to keep it for him. For safety she dropped it into one of his boots which he had set beside her. When he came out of the water, he shouted to her to throw him his boots, as the shore was pebbly, and she flung them towards him with all her strength, never thinking of the ring. When he was dressed and sitting beside her again with his boots on, he asked her for it and all the horror of what she had done rushed into her mind. She felt sure that in the precarious state of his brain he would look upon the loss as symbolic and be driven completely out of his senses. She put up a despairing cry to God, at the same moment laying her fingers on the sand beside her, and they closed over the ring.

Tuesday May 19, 1942 – Georgia's birthday

Last Wednesday, May 20, I had my first Italian lesson from Francesco. The thought came to me when I saw how frightened he was at the prospect of the doctor's bill – for he has had to go up to London three times a week for treatment, and Mother entirely approved. I know by Eileen Bowen Davies, who objected to paying it, that he charges 10/- for a lesson in composition, so I took a cheque for Mother of £5. [53] He didn't want to take it, at any rate till we saw if he was any use to me, but

53 This suggests that even at the age of 67 Mabel did not have full control of the family finances.

I left it on the dressing table. The table in his room was covered with music paper, inscribed in the tiniest neatest writing. This was Mrs Van der Elst's Symphony. He told me he felt himself most lucky, for she is so pleased with their joint compositions that she intends to get together a full orchestra and have them performed. Francesco says it is the dream of every composer to have his works played. But I said, *"It will be under her name, not yours"*, *"What does that matter?"* he asked. She had given him a series of notes, about one line of the music paper, and as he was harmonising it. Another and very pleasing phrase came to him which he worked into the first and played over to her and she instantly and innocently accepted it as hers and was delighted. I don't like the whole thing very much, but Noel thinks it is quite legitimate.

Friday May 29, 1942

Last Wednesday as I was leaving for my lesson, I saw a baby thrush on the path near the kitchen window. I was afraid it was injured as it seemed unable either to hop or fly. It kept quite quiet and never cheeped as I passed by. It was still there when I came back. A wild night of wind and rain was setting in, so wild that Millicent tells me she and her neighbours had little sleep, and feared that their windows would be blown in. I couldn't leave the little bird unsheltered in the cold and placed him in my bicycle basket well steeped with warm lining, he protested lustily as he lay in my hands. I got a little water down his throat, but he refused to open his mouth either for soaked bread or worms (I put two worms in a cup but when I returned after a short absence I found the cup empty. I fear its occupants are still at loose on the carpet). He slept I think without waking – indeed I had little doubt he was dead – till the birds began to sing outside a little before five. Then his chirps became more and more frequent and I lifted up the basket to try once more to feed him, but in vain. I found him however full of life and enterprise. He gripped my finger with both his feet and absolutely refused to stay in his basket, so there was nothing for it but to restore him to the garden and let him try to summon his parents. There was a slight drizzle falling but it soon cleared and I was able to find a sheltered spot under a hedge on short grass. This time he never cheeped while I lifted and carried him and seemed quite happy in my protection. This was about 5.30pm and until 7.30pm his cries had no effect. I saw sparrows and a blackbird come to investigate and presently a small thrush flew across the lawn and began to peck about near the baby, looking at him over her shoulder, but alas swallowing the worms that came abundantly to her beak. But what was my joy at last to find her feeding him and evidently interlarding her worms with parental advice, for very shortly he had hopped away into the undergrowth at the side of the rock garden and when I looked for him again at dinner time he was no more to be seen.

We have had Lucy Knowles from Saturday to Tuesday – a most happy visit and a great help to me. For she dusted Mother's room and I was able to go out almost at once to weed in the garden. I had three barrow loads of weeds to show for my morning's work and was thankful again for Lucy's kindness, which allowed me to spend the rest of the day in bed, to recover from these exertions!

Thursday June 4, 1942

When I arrived for my lesson, I heard Francesco practising and I asked if it was allowed. He said no, but he must practise, as he is playing at a concert in Liverpool [54] on the 24th and at another in London on July 19th. [55] His arm always pains him after playing, but fortunately not at the time. I feel very anxious about it, remembering Arnold Clibborn, [56] who had to drop playing altogether after three years study to be a professional pianist. I don't think we know anyone in Liverpool we could tell about it. I am afraid Jo and Arnold [57] are much too far away. I asked him to come to lunch with Mrs Pearce on the Sunday after your [58] birthday, to meet Noel and he was pleased, but I didn't see Mrs Pearce. They won't arrive till 1.20pm, as Francesco plays at the Free Church, but that will suit me very well. We will all rest in the afternoon. We had tea and our lesson at the far end of the garden under some trees – even so it was very hot. I was too hot last night,

54 Mabel had made a note of Francesco's concert date: *"June 24 1942 Crane Hall, Liverpool, Piano only. 12–1. Same programme 1–2"*.

55 Mabel had made a note of Francesco's other concert date: *"July 19 1942 Warwick Theatre London 6pm. Mixed Concert got up by the violinist Angel Grande. Francesco plays a violin and piano sonata with Grande and a group of solo pieces by Chopin"*.

56 Clibborn, Arnold (1883-1964), family friend.

57 The aforementioned Arnold Clibborn and his wife.

58 Her Mother, Clara.

sleeping in the verandah, with only one blanket on. I was hoping to have a little time with Mrs Pearce – she teaches in a school where they give her tea, but she said she would be home about quarter to six, but we could hear continuous lessons going on after that. I suppose she saw we were deep in our work and wouldn't come out. Francesco had to go to catch a train at 6.15pm and I waited about for a while, hoping Mrs Pearce's pupil would go but it was I who went in the end. I think she works far too hard and on such exacting work. I suppose she must do it, to make a living.

Sunday June 7, 1942

Noel is to broadcast on the 19th on Rousseau.

Je suis Jean – Je suis Jacques
Je suis Roux – Je suis Sot
Mais je ne suis pas Jean Jacques Rousseau.

This, according to Francesco, was an epigram made on the spot about some red-headed man of the same Christian names as the famous one.

I have had two very interesting Sunday afternoons thanks to Miss Barnes, who is taking tomorrow to go to London instead, and buy a hat. Last week at three was Mr Milburn's paper on *"Reconstruction"*. He set out a proposal for a super-Church after the war, to unite all God-fearing people irrespective of Creed. As I had been told, the best part of the afternoon came with the discussion as we sat round the tea table prepared by Francesco and myself. There were present an Austrian Doctor (of philosophy I think) [59] and his wife, who speaks very imperfect English, but writes such good novels in German that they are exported to America and translated there. They were both quite young, eager looking with typical German faces. A discussion arose between the man and Francesco, both speaking the most excellent English: the Austrian doctor's was practically faultless, tho' his wife pulled him up for gesticulating. He told us of the rotten state of France before the War, and put it down to their complete loss of faith. Francesco was talking chiefly of the effect of Roman Catholic teaching – a subject which always drives him beside himself – but what I chiefly

59 Mabel's note at the top of the page "Dr. Kineti – spelling unknown". His name was Elias Canetti (1905–1994). He was a European refugee billeted with Mr Milburn. Both men were authors. Canetti won the Nobel Prize for literature in 1981.

remember is his *"No, no, no, no, no, no!"* to some statement of the other doctor's. There won't be another meeting till September, when Noel is to be the speaker. Yesterday was a programme given at the little Repertory Theatre [60] on Station Road by pupils and friends of Georgia's and largely consisted of her own music. The highlights for me were the Recitations by Stella Newton, Georgia's daughter, and the singing of Mrs Lilienfeld, who has a glorious voice, great avvenenza [61] and a most charming exterior. She is evidently a very practised singer. Francesco says she has been a professional. It seems sad that she should be married to an arrogant looking Jew stockbroker, of twice her age, though he is to be sure, a passionate music lover and plays very well, I think, the violin. I went early to the Studio and watered my marrows and helped a little in the kitchen. Meeting Stella at the back door, she said *"I think you must be "our Miss Brailsford!"*. I had the pleasure of walking with *"Stella"* to the theatre – the others came in Mr Sloley's car, with a bust of Shakespeare that stood on the stage throughout. I stayed a while in the dressing room, where I saw *"Stella"* and Mary Evans, who was to dance or rather posture to music, dressing and making up. She has a very charming peaceful face. Georgia says she is a saint. She is a member of the queer Church in London that Georgia goes to. [62] Francesco had asked me to keep a seat for him as he could only arrive at the last minute, and I found places for all of us near the front. Eric Newton [63] and Mr Sloley sitting in front of Francesco. Connie (his French pupil with whom he arrived) and myself. Tea was brought round at half-time – it was a comic little War touch that Connie had my lump of sugar, which I don't take, and also .....

[unfinished]

60 The Playhouse, Station Road, Amersham.
61 Italian: *beauty.*
62 Order of the Cross.
63 Stella's husband. Mrs Pearce's son-in-law.

Friday July 3, 1942

I am very sorry I have had no time to keep this book written up. I have been in London again for the day, in a desperate attempt to get a birthday present, in which I was successful. I got her [64] at Foyles [65] three French books in the Nelson edition, which cost 2/6 each and used to be 2/-. Noel (with Clare's 10/- to help him) got a masculine umbrella, which I have screwed on to the stand made for it when Mung was here. I don't think we ever had a happier birthday than last Saturday – her 99th! [66] I should say the umbrella – not a silk one – cost 23/6 and was the last but one in a huge shop in Finchley Road [67]. I had searched London and Amersham in vain. I suppose no more will be made – partly because the materials are needed for munitions and partly because most of the population is in uniform – but what about the old gentlemen who always were the chief umbrella carriers?

Then on Sunday – just a week ago – we had Georgia and Francesco to lunch. It was a lovely day. I hurried home from playing at the Chapel [68] and set the big garden table at the end of the little terrace near the wild cherry. Mother lay beside it on the garden couch, facing towards the glorious riot of roses in the two big beds under the windows. They were at the height of their beauty for her birthday. That day Mrs Barrett [69] had been the first to arrive, with a lovely bunch of roses and two of her own eggs. Soon after came Mrs Essex [70], with a most tasteful tight Victorian bouquet (a beaupot I think it should be called) carried by her little Norman of three. Mrs Exell came later with more roses from Little Elms [71], that she always brings to Mother on her birthday.
I haven't recorded that a week ago we had an afternoon with Mrs Lilienfeld – tea in the garden and singing afterwards. Mother heard her beautifully as she held the tube with one hand and sang into it. It was all too short and it was not till she was going that I knew she had brought two songs of Francesco's, and we had not tried them. However

64 Her Mother, Clara.
65 Foyles is a bookshop in Charing Cross Road, London.
66 Her Mother, Clara.
67 Finchley Road, London.
68 Mabel played the piano during services at the Methodist Church, High Street, Amersham.
69 Neighbour from 'Malvern', London Road.
70 Neighbour from 'Stonygreen', London Road.
71 This was the house Mabel and her Mother first lived in when they came to Amersham.

she is to come once a week to tea and practise. I was telling him I had just had the handsome sum of 3/- as six months Royalties on Susanna [72], but he said he could beat that, as he has just received 4d on the sale of one of his songs – and that represented his profit on one he had happened to buy himself! When he and Georgia were hoping to have a Musical Festival in August, she said she wanted him to write the opening chorus and he turned to me and asked me to write the words. I have done a very free adaptation of Luther's Frau Musika – it came to me straight off after I had read the poems – so I hoped it didn't creak in the joints. I read it aloud when we were sitting round the table and to my joy and surprise Noel exclaimed, *"You have done that extremely well, Mabel"*. I gave the paper to Francesco and he studied it with the original, but said nothing at all till I went to my lesson on Tuesday, when it seems to me he thought far too highly of it and of the evangelii [73] that it came from. He didn't like one word – ugly - *"Nor any ugly thing"* which I had rather fancied. However now that I have altered it to hurtful I see he is right. But in the end he preferred to let it stand and has been working on the music all last Sunday. I took their photographs after lunch – and one of Francesco after he had fallen fast asleep in his chair. Georgia was slumbering in hers and Noel snoring in my bedroom. On the day before, Georgia had had seventeen *"members of the Order"* from London and gave them tea – all on her own. Francesco as always was in town and got home unusually late: but she was glad, for she is trying to attract him to the Order and thought these very dull narrow and excellent people would not have helped. He could not read the textbook of the Order because it is written in such bad English – O how I sympathise! One of them, an old pupil whom I used to know as Bertha, stayed over Sunday night, at her own invitation, so Georgia had to go back by the 4.30pm bus to give her tea. Francesco stayed till the 5.30pm which gave him time to get to his Free Church – talking with Noel. Noel said when he was going he was disappointed not to have had any music – so he asked us to go up after supper. It was a glorious moonlight night, the moon hanging very low in the sky and looking twice her usual size as we walked home towards

72 Mabel's book: *"Susanna Wesley, the mother of Methodism"*. 1910.

73 Gospel.

her. For we had to walk both ways – two buses in succession rushing past us on the way there – and no taxi being willing to fetch us home. Noel was terribly tired, for he hasn't recovered from his 'flu and his three trials of bicycling, but the music atoned for everything. It was chiefly on the two grand pianos which had just been tuned and sounded like one instrument. First two pieces of Francesco's on Bells – which I found interesting and ingenious, but not at all moving – and then a Chorale, followed by a Sarabande, both most tuneful, but packed with thought and full of interesting harmonies and progressions. Francesco was to play something alone afterwards and I asked for the little Liszt Eclogue, which was the first thing he ever played me and which I love for that reason. But all the glamour had gone out of it when one contrasted it with Francesco's own work: and to my joy Noel made much the same comment, saying it was a charming thing but nothing like as interesting and thoughtful as what had gone before. (On Thursday when I went for my lesson I heard what I thought was the piano tuner, but it was Francesco, practising (in his shirt sleeves) one note, over and over – to get the exact tone.)

For a long time we haven't been able to buy anything to clean the saucepans with, as all metal is commandeered for munitions. Yesterday when I was washing up I found to my delight a most elegant pancleaner and asked Mrs Pearce about it. She said her daughter had found it in London and given it to Francesco as a present! He does all the washing up.

Friday July 17, 1942

Miss Barnes is in London with her brother for two weeks holiday, so I told her this story and asked her to look out for a similar cleaner. Her remark was: *"Fancy a man washing up. I suppose foreigners do that sort of thing!"*. She never loses an opportunity of getting her knife into Mrs Pearce. When I told her my pie had been greatly appreciated and that everyone had had second helps, she rejoined, *"Yes, I imagine Mrs Pearce would have a second help."* I felt mad and asked her very quietly *"What exactly do you mean by that, Miss Barnes?"* Whereupon she very meekly climbed down, saying *"I only mean it was a very nice pie."*

Well Miss Barnes being away Francesco came to give me my lesson [74]. Mother was in bed, having caught a slight cold, and he carried in her tea. He seems to be always carrying trays – as a visiting American friend wrote the other day to Mr Sloley – *"in a pontifical manner"*. We had a long talk over tea, in English – though since he accused me of being *"pigra"* [75]. I am learning to speak Italian at every opportunity. I wanted to know what he felt about the Universal Church, that Mr Milburn had been describing on the other Sunday afternoon. He told me amongst other things, that one of the enlightened Jews at the Synagogue where he plays, had proposed that their day of worship should be changed to Sunday as, said he, they lost the help and influence of the innumerable acts of worship that went on on that day. His proposal was of course turned down, with the question *"Why don't you propose that we should turn Christians altogether?" "O no,"* said the first man, *"that we could never do, as we don't believe in the Trinity."* I wonder how many *"Christians"* could lay their hands on their hearts and say that they believed in it.

Francesco has an obsession about Everlasting punishment and has twice told me how the priest dinned into him as a tiny boy – *"You have once burned your finger and you remember how it hurt? Hell will be ten times worse and it will last, not for ten minutes, not for an hour, not for a day, not for a year, not for 100 years, but for ever and ever and ever"*. He asked a good clergyman the other day if he was able to believe in Hell, as his duty compelled him. *"O Yes,"* he replied, *"I do believe there is a Hell, but I don't believe there is any one in it!"*

Alas for Francesco's hopes of hearing his music performed (under the name of Mrs Van der Elst) that lady has been frequenting some séances and the medium told her to have no more to do with it – so she has dropped out altogether and doesn't let herself be heard of. It is a great loss financially, but none of us are sorry. It wasn't a true situation and as Georgia told him, could never lead to good.

74 By this time it appears that Miss Barnes, Mabel's live-in refugee, is acting as a 'sitter' for Mabel's mother which explains why Mabel is able to spend so much time at the Music Studio. In Miss Barnes absence Mabel is effectively 'grounded'.

75 Italian: lazy

We have had two bitter days of wind and almost incessant rain – the thermometer never rising above sixty. Poor Miss Barnes, and poor Georgia – who has gone with her daughter to Torquay for the inside of a week. Francesco will teach her pupils. Susan [76] and I have been in the garden picking quantities of the rasps that would otherwise have fallen. There is a wonderful crop on both the old and new bushes and for some reason the birds are not taking toll of them though I have left them uncovered.

Wednesday July 22, 1942

Riding home from chapel last Sunday, I had just entered the narrower part of High Street when I saw a little bird hit by a motor as it flew across towards the Church. It twitched once, and then lay flat on the ground with both wings outspread. I got off and picked it up, to save it being run over again by the next car, but not knowing if it was dead or alive. But it gripped my finger with its little claws, as though to say, *"Thank you, I know I am safe now."* I brought it home in my bicycle basket, lying on and covered by my waterproof, and left the whole affair in the garden while I got the dinner. It refused all food. The first time I looked at it it had turned right round and was standing up – a beautiful young swallow with a back like mackerel and a velvet head. When I went after dinner the basket was empty.

On Monday the telephone authorities put us in a new telephone, saying our own was obsolete. It had been growing very faint especially for long distance calls, and the first use of it was made that night, when the bell woke me from my first sleep at 10.30pm. It was Adelaide, speaking from London, where she is having a very short holiday away from Oldham, where she is leading a very sad and devoted life in attendance upon Mary, who is nearly blind. She proposed to come out to tea yesterday, but I begged her to come for the night, and stay over this morning as Francesco would be here for lunch and stay to give me my lesson. So I got Miss Barnes' bed ready for myself, and we have had

76 Mabel's dog.

a most happy time. It was a wonderful stroke of luck that Miss Barnes should be away. We gathered the dinner that evening: beans, new potatoes, and a great bowl of raspberries, and I made parsley sauce and a semolina cheese. I think everyone enjoyed the meeting as much as I did, talking Italian most of the time. Francesco told us he had had a most interesting weekend. He was staying at the house of a plate-layer (I think it was – or a signalman) on the railway line with whom his own boy [77] had made friends. The man is passionately fond of music and plays the violin and viola, while his son plays the 'cello. They took in (from a newspaper advertisement) a young Austrian girl who plays the piano extremely well and they have concerts together. When Francesco arrived, he was presented with the programme of a Concert to be held that evening in the Library of his own boy's public school near by – *"Music by Ticciati"*. There were songs, violin pieces, and a piano concerto all written by this boy of nineteen, who has never, Francesco says, had a music lesson. The explanation of this strange fact is that the boy is equally brilliant in languages and literature and the headmaster has consistently discouraged his musical side, wishing him to bring honour to the school in public exams. It was only the encouragement and insistence of all the other Masters, that brought this concert to pass. The boy was expected to take a high scholarship to Oxford but because of his addiction to music he has only got an Exhibition – this does mean some sort of scholarship, I think? He is staying on near the school, having found himself pupils for coaching. This will keep him till the war is over, when his Exhibition will take him to Worcester College, Oxford. Francesco says, jokingly, that they must come to some sort of arrangement about their names, appended to their compositions! I think it gave him a little shock to see the name of *"Ticciati"* tout court [78], at the top of a programme with which he had nothing to do!

77 Niso Ticciati.
78 French: simply.

Friday July 24, 1942

I had such a huge washing today. I didn't want to tell you [79] till it was all dry, starched and ironed – 5.45pm!

Two silk nightdresses of yours: two woolly coats
One cotton nightdress – MRB – not ironable
One silk petticoat
One silk knickers
Two cotton coms
One flowery teacloth Mab Keogh – ironed only.
Three serviettes starched and ironed
One small tablecloth, starched and ironed
The print frock I have been wearing
One small apron
One handkerchief of Adelaide's
One roller towel
One huckaback towel
And a few old dusters etc I found dirty. [80]

Thursday July 30, 1942

I had my usual luck in the weather, for it had been raining all morning and just stopped, as I set out for the Studio at 12.30pm. The wind too blew me up the hill. I heard Francesco practising arpeggios as I arrived and Georgia was in the kitchen, putting finishing touches to the dinner. I wanted to stay to help her, but she asked me to go in and talk to him – anything to stop him practicing so that she could attend to the cooking. She said she couldn't help listening and taking her mind off the dishes, for all her life it had been her duty to listen to pupils performing the same. So he did stop, and began telling me at once of the song he had just composed. He said, and of course we know it is true, that he doesn't think highly of himself but he felt that this time he had given the best that is in him. He was in a very excited exalté state of mind. It seems my poem is to open the concert, and they were searching for another to close it and could find nothing. At last they

79 Her Mother, Clara.
80 MAB (Mab Keogh) was a deceased friend and relative and Mabel had inherited her house and contents. There are no sheets and pillowcases in this list so they must use a laundry service for these.

got Gertrude Bone's little book, *"The Hidden Orchis"* which I gave Georgia for her birthday and when Francesco got to the last page he found this poem which seemed to him what he had been waiting for all his life. He wanted to know if she was as beautiful a character as her writing. I told him all I could about her, but when I looked at the book I saw it was a poem by Gavin [81], and not by her at all. This seemed to me a most beautiful thing if I would tell Gertrude and Muirhead how Gavin's work had inspired a great artist to what he feels to be his best work, but Francesco was deeply disappointed that he was dead – he had hoped they could have gone on collaborating. At this point he played me the two songs – both I thought, exquisite in very different ways. My Frau Musika is like laughing water, but it is most varied, following very closely the sense of the verses – now gay, now very quaint, reminding one of Handel – and ending most surprisingly in a solemn chorale, to suit the words *"But chiefly to our God ....".* Francesco was so happy because he says he has been longing for months and months to compose and never met anything that could inspire him and Gavin's poem was ideal.

At this point we had lunch and before we had finished *"Freda"* came in [82]. She is one of the ladies with whom Francesco lived and from whom Mrs Black rescued him, after *"three major rows"* in one week. I wasn't expecting to like her, but I did. She is most evidently a great artist herself, with a wonderful voice and an equally wonderful technique. Only the last month or so she has reconciled herself with Francesco. She must have passed a most unhappy year, for she is soaked in his music and after a while she consented to sing first one and then another of his songs – neither of them having any music. The second one – a Spring song – she said always bought down the house, but no accompanist could tackle the accompaniment at sight, and for this reason no publisher will publish it. Then it was 3 o'clock and a singing pupil arrived who is being trained in voice production by Georgia and *"Freda"* (I don't know her other name, it is foreign and she is a Jewess) [83] so we went to Francesco's room for our Italian lesson.

81 Gavin Bone (1907-1942), artist, writer, academician. Son of Muirhead and Gertrude Bone.
82 Frida Dancyger (1888-1970). Singer.
83 Mabel added *"Dantziger"* later, although misspelled it was phonetically correct.

Very shortly after I saw Mr. Fountain's head [84] through the window and Mr Sloley, who has been trying to tinker the clock himself, arrived for a consultation! I wanted Francesco to meet Mr Fountain and have a talk about music, but I couldn't persuade him. He says I have no idea what an ordeal it is for him to meet a new person and have to talk. The sun had come out and we found that we were all to have tea in the garden. We had most interesting talk all the time, partly about Francesco's first days in London, when he was taking English lessons from *"Violet"*. [85] She gave him tongue exercises to conquer the English *th* and he used to practice them and his finger exercises in the London buses, much to Freda's embarrassment, who was often sitting with him on the same journey. He was altogether so full of fun today – he has alas to register for National Service this week and gave us a description of his experiences on the last occasion. He was kept waiting an hour, and no one could tell him where to go to – though one official directed him to the office for Old Age Pensions!!! (of course this was an invention!) He talked a good deal about Macbeth, *"Freda"* maintaining that Lady Macbeth was a strong character.

Sunday August 2, 1942

(Seven years today since Mab Keogh died)

I have just heard on the Wireless that the British Government has asked all British subjects, men and women, to return from the U.S.A., unless they are already engaged on work of national importance. Their fares will be paid.

Tuesday August 4, 1942

Francesco came again today at his own request for lunch and our lesson on the verandah. He wanted to help me to wash up, but of course Miss Barnes was here to do it. [86] We had so many interesting talks today, arising out of what we were reading. For instance the short story I translate is about a man in lodgings in Florence with a landlady who had such a gift for racy and picturesque speech that the author

84 There was a Mr Fountain, a gardener, and also one who had a cycle repair shop in the High Street.

85 Defries.

86 Mabel appears to be treating Miss Barnes as the live-in help!

learnt more from her in a couple of weeks than in ten years from his professor. I wondered why an Italian should have ten years coaching in Italian. Francesco says an Italian audience is terribly critical of language in orators – cruel he said – an orator might be hissed off the platform for an inelegant sentence, regardless of his learning or earnestness.

Frau Musika

Of all the joys on earth
Than those we share in song
No finer can there be
And all sweet melody

No evil tempers live
No anger, envy, hate
Where friends in concert sing
No care for the morrow
Nor any ugly thing –
Nor any sorrow

Ours is the sweet of the year
With song the woods are full
All thanks to them we pay
When all the small birds sing
And even the sky doth sing
With their sweet lay

But chiefly to our God
Who made them thus, to be
His Master Choristers,
And praise Him, even as we
Who chant His praise,
And thank him, all our days.

Very frei nach [87] *Martin Luther*

Francesco told me he had had a great longing to write, but has never been able to satisfy himself. He told me today he had written, or did write, verse. I hope he will show me some. I told him I had written to Gertrude asking her and Muirhead to come to the Concert in September. He had forgotten that he had to get back for a lesson to Dr. Robinson, and to give him tea and was in trouble about the cakes, but I made a big batch of scones this morning and wrapped up ten of them and put them in his pocket. We didn't think Dr. Robinson need see him abstract them!

87 German: freely adapted from.

Sunday August 9, 1942

Double Summer Time ends.

This was the queerest and longest Sunday I ever spent! I couldn't sleep the extra hour due to us, so I got up at seven by old time, six by new. Miss Barnes of course sleeps through anything for as long as you like. We wanted our breakfast presently, so I got it, and had it cleared away by the time Miss Barnes awoke – 8.30am I think by the new time. Mrs Pearce had told me on the telephone the night before, that Francesco was down with a baddish attack of flu, but he had given Connie her French lesson as usual on the Friday – very bad for him and for her too I should think. *"Freda"* goes to the studio on Thursday to give a lesson in voice production and finding him ill she wrote to Mrs Pearce who came straight home, losing a week end of the Convocation to which she has been looking forward for months. I felt anxious about her as she is not strong enough for any extra work and I went up there about 9.30am, thanks to the extra hour. It was well timed for Georgia had just cleared away the breakfast things and I was beginning to wash up the accumulation from supper, when she appeared in her dressing gown. She wouldn't let me wash up, as the little girl Dorothy was coming, but gave me an apron and a duster and asked me to dust the music room. The sun was pouring into the open French window and she had laid the garden mattress and a pillow on the carpet, for him to lie on when he came out of the bath. Presently she helped him in – very cheerful but horribly weak. She went then to have her bath and left me to talk to him. I had brought a nice basketful of the first of our apples and I sat on a stool just outside the window in the sun peeling them till she joined us. When I left at twenty to eleven for the service the sun was still shining but it felt and looked very thundery. I flew down the steep Rectory Hill (where they had held a Fete the day before, in almost incessant rain) and it had come on again before the service was well begun. Mr. Clegg told me that he had heard again from his boy in Libya – a wire and two letters. He is only twenty two and was a schoolboy when he last saw him – now for some weeks he has been Acting-Major, in the absence of two of his superiors. I rode home through cataracts of rain to find Miss Barnes most unpleasant as always, at my having gone to help Mrs Pearce. *"You shouldn't have gone rushing up the hill like that to nurse a sick man!"* I remarked mildly that I didn't go to nurse a sick man, but to be of any help I could to Mrs Pearce. *"She ought to send him to a nursing home if she can't manage without calling on her friends to help her. I nursed my Mother for (so long) and I never asked anyone to help me ..."* and so on and so forth. She says she can't imagine anyone wanting to learn Italian now – she won't want to speak to an Italian or a German for many a year! *"They are all the same!"* Poor Miss Barnes. It was as well that she was out when Mr and Mrs Lilienfeld turned up about six and joined us on the verandah. I had been expecting her to ring me up in ten days to arrange to come for a practice, but six weeks had passed and she was full of apologies. He was very pleasant and full of interest in Mother and delight in our little home. Susan [88] came to investigate him and he began to make squeaky noises with his palms pressed together, to perplex her. He went on to play a whole tune – God Save the King – by the same action, then the Marseillaise, and finally I held Mother's tube to his hands and she distinctly recognised the tune. He says when he was young his sister came back from South Africa with the trick of making single notes in this way and he has practised and developed it. He needs very clean hands and sometimes powders the palms and can play thus with an orchestra.

We have just heard that Mr Churchill has been in Moscow this week, consulting with Stalin. American army chiefs were at the meeting and our General Warde.

Monday 24 August, 1942

I have just realised what a sunless summer this has been, from the fact that I have never needed to darken the windows in the larder. In normal Junes and Julys the early morning sun pours in there, to the detriment of whatever may be upon the shelves. It is an unpleasant summer too for the multitude of earwigs and wasps. I have just had the third sting in ten days upon my right arm, and a very pretty heavily laden tree of red apples has been almost gutted, the apples still hanging there round and red but completely empty.

88 Mabel's dog.

Monday 31 August, 1942

So ends this summer and my book [89] together. Last Friday night I had an altogether new pleasure at the Studio. Connie's matric is to be tomorrow week, and a tiny group of friends was assembled in the evening to read As You Like It. Mr Sloley was there and the only dull reader. A man and wife, pupils of Georgia's – he is quite young and quite blind with the sweetest happiest face, full of laughter. He was sorry he could not join in the Shakespeare reading, not having brought his Braille copy. Georgia says he is a very fine singer and organist and his wife, very much older than he, very stout and very much made up, is a professional singer. Francesco is rehearsing every day almost all day for the Concert of his and Georgia's music on the 19th at the house of Eric and Stella Newton. His music to Gertrude Bone's poem is terribly difficult and most enchanting. Mr Lilienfeld comes here to practice on many mornings – I couldn't remember any of the passages when I tried – they are so strange and difficult, but last night the one I like best came to me in my sleep and returned again during the morning. The reading lasted till 10.30pm and I did not get home till after 11pm. The walk home was most delightful by broad moonlight. Francesco walked with Connie and me through the dark lanes to the road and then we went on together to Black Horse Bridge. My way took me down Stanley Hill, past the wood where an owl was tewhit tewhooing. Mother hadn't tried to sleep and was full of interest and sympathy in my adventures. She slept nearly all the next morning, so there was no harm done.

I have been up to examine the loft above the Studio [90] and found there a very nice rug (with moths in it) and a campbed.

Thursday 3 September, 1942

This is the Day of Prayer at the opening of the fourth year of the War. I am afraid since my own life became so interesting, this record has been little but a private diary of no interest as a sidelight on the War. But indeed in this little town twenty five miles from London we might be 1000 miles from any scene of conflict. We had one warning about a

89 Last page of exercise book in which the diary is written.
90 Mrs Pearce's Music Studio.

week ago and heard the sound of distant gunfire, and during the last full moon we heard an occasional German plane overhead and had a warning on several nights. But Amersham streets are almost like themselves again since the Evacuees began going back in shoals to their homes. Mrs Coleman's refugee has returned to Ealing with Bobby and found a job at Munitions. Miss Bush has had to return to her flat in Chiswick, following her school, which has been dis-evacuated. Mrs Glover too is living in Chiswick for the week, but intends to return to her own house for week-ends. For all this, the Lewises and little Dr. Morley Davies have failed so far to find new billets for them, and she talks of returning to London ….. I am very far from happy about Mrs Pearce and am afraid she will break down and be finally unable to carry on. The relations between herself and Francesco are quite as happy and unclouded as ever, yet many outside things are pressing in and complicating the situation. Perhaps the worst is that he is no longer able to practise at the Blacks, where he used to spend three hours every morning on his own piano. Their neighbour, an old lady inclined to hysteria, has protested that she can't endure it. So now he practises in the Studio. Georgia has trained herself as her life work to listen critically to music and focus all her attention on what is being played. She can't now break the habit even if she wished. The result is that she can concentrate on nothing either cooking or her own practising and feels that she is growing more and more nervy. "Freda" (Danziger) is perhaps the greatest complication – now that she has made it up with Francesco she seems to be never out of the house. She is a woman with no reticence and flaunts their friendship before strangers in season and out of season. So poor Georgia has too much Freda and no peace. At the At Home on the Sunday (to which I didn't go and I am glad now that I didn't) she came very late and simply put her head round the door and beckoned to Francesco. He went, as Georgia says, like a lamb and stayed out of the room for half an hour. Again at a Reception given in his honour, when everyone was crowding round to speak to him, she put her arm through his and drags him away, saying she was tired. Georgia is very upset about it as she fears he will get a bad reputation, which is the last thing he deserves. When Georgia told me this, I said the one hope is that she should quarrel with him again, but she looked so shocked and said we must never wish for that. She told me then that soon after Francesco came to live at the Studio, Freda came to see her and abused her up hill and down dale for stealing him away. She was so violent that Georgia became ill. In the afternoon she came back and said she was sorry and ever since Georgia has felt that she must do all in her power to help her. I can't see any way out, unless she and her Aunt go back to London as I suppose they will when the War ends. Georgia thinks Francesco is very fond of her but I am sure she is wrong. He is very loyal and habit is very strong and he has a great admiration for her singing and gratitude for her interpretation of his song. But one evening he had an appointment to go with her to the theatre and stayed talking in the kitchen after our lesson till the very last minute when he explained "*Well I must leave you – con – molto dispiacere* – "[91]. I overtook them on the Station Hill walking side by side - he was reading a paper.

I had two strange nights this week. In the first, the chief phrase of Francesco's setting of Gertrude's poem, comes back to me, though I have always tried in vain to remember it. In the second, I woke at three with the plan, cut and dried, of lending our hall Cosy Stove for Francesco's room. I could hardly restrain myself from ringing them up at that hour, for in the afternoon I had been up the ladder to look in the loft for a fireplace which should have been there and was not. I went round by 9 o'clock next morning and found Georgia lying ill in bed with heart trouble. Francesco was in London to play at his synagogue. I think she needed more than anything else to pour out her troubles and anxieties. I made her bed, and dusted the Studio when she got up, and persuaded her to come to us for the whole of tomorrow. She wouldn't stay the night – she says she will have the Studio to herself on Sunday morning to do as she likes.

91 Italian: with much regret.

Friday 4 September, 1942

I have just come home from a Concert given entirely by the blind man and his wife (Mr and Mrs Burrows) whom I met at the reading of As You Like It. The three ladies were still rehearsing with Francesco when I arrived – it was his song, The Traveller, set to words of Rabindranath Tagore. They had been at it since ten o'clock. I listened for five minutes and then went to finish getting tea in the kitchen. Every time I do it I think of Werther *"had a love for Charlotte / that his tongue could never utter / Would you know how first he met her? / She was cutting bread and butter."* [92] I was cutting up some very fat sort of scones, splitting and buttering them. Francesco came in and I consulted him whether this was the best way. He said he thought it was better to cut them in three *"but of course,"* he said, *"it depends on the elasticity of the people's mouths."* People were coming in now and I thought he ought to go and help to receive them. I got a seat on the divan next to Mrs Lilienfeld and Mrs Downer, whose baby I accommodated with a stool at her feet. She sat so quiet and good, having already had two hours of the rehearsal, but when one of the audience commended her and asked if she had enjoyed the music, she gave an emphatic no! Mr Burrows and his wife divided the programme – at least he was always at the piano either solo, or accompaniment, except for Mr Sloley's cycle of five songs, for which Georgia played. I thoroughly enjoyed these songs – they were most melodious and beautifully harmonized. They all dealt with some aspect of India. Mrs Burrows (Carol Squire) has a very lovely sweet high soprano, under perfect control. At this point an extraordinary figure came in – a very good-looking young woman with a look at once blank and intense if you can imagine it. She was dressed (to begin at the top) in a big bandanna handkerchief on her head the point hanging down her back and half concealing a long lock of hair which nearly reached her waist. Over a light blouse she wore a long black coat like a man's overcoat and (I think brown corduroy) trousers, ending in open sandals and bare feet. She carried a very long and thick stick, like an alpenstock, with a knob at the top. When Mr Burrows played a very loud and brilliant polonaise of Chopin's, this Miss Alexander got up and went out leaving this implement lying full

92 Thackeray, William Makepeace. The Sorrows of Werther.

in the passage way for the blind man to fall over, if another of the audience had not seen it and removed it. I gathered afterwards that she was suffering from nerves. If I was her doctor, I should first of all insist on her wearing the same get up as other people. It would be a terrible strain on anybody to go about in that guise. She is very good looking too. Also after tea, she smoked two or three cigarettes at once! Tea was great fun – the three men sat at the far end of the table and I between Georgia and Mrs Burrows. Francesco entertained the blind pianist and constant laughter came from their end. Afterwards we cleared away and Mrs Burrows insisted on helping me to wash up and made such a good job of it – drying every cup instead of leaving it to drain, as Francesco always does. I stayed just a little while longer for it was so interesting. The two pianists were comparing notes and Francesco would suddenly sit down and dash off the most devastatingly difficult passage and then Mr Burrows would try over something he had heard Francesco play – in his tempo. He asked Francesco if he had every written a Concerto for piano and orchestra and Francesco sat down and played a few dozen most brilliant bars – acknowledging, after questioning, that he had played it four times at the Queen's Hall under Sir Henry Wood at the Philharmonic Concerts, and once in Rome. Then I went, and Georgia took Mrs Burrows into the little Studio (Francesco's room) to practise the three songs of her composing that Mrs Burrows is to sing on the 19th.

– on Saturday Georgia spent the day with us and Francesco came for her about eight and they walked home – a most happy time.

Monday 7 September, 1942

A letter inserted in the diary from Noel Brailsford to Mabel.

My Dear Mab,

I've been down with flu' and in bed, but I'm better now. I want to thank both you and Mother for your letters—and you for the always welcome watch box. My subject will be *"Gerrard Winstanley the Light Shining in Buckinghamshire."* And now I hope I won't disappoint you. I had meant to come down to you on Friday or Saturday the 25th or 26th, but the Fabian Society wants my help at a weekend conference about India which it is holding in Oxford from that Friday to Sunday.

As you may realise I care deeply about India, and so have accepted on condition that they'll get me somehow to Amersham by Sunday morning. But en revanche [93]; I can stay, if I may, with you and Mother over Monday. I do hope this doesn't put you out. Yes I'll go to the Newton's on the 19th. With much love to you both, Noel.

Tell Mother I shall have an article in the New Statesman about Laxton which will explain what 'open fields' are—or were.

Wednesday September 9, 1942

I went to the Studio about three to plant out two dozen of Frank Johnston's Russian Kale. Georgia and "Freda" were teaching a young married pupil singing and voice production. It is wonderfully generous of Georgia to share her pupil and with a woman she can't love. Then Mrs Downer and the baby Janet arrived for her lesson and they stayed to tea, which I got ready and sat in the garden. She has a beautiful cultivated voice and sings with her whole heart. She is the third of Francesco's trio. Francesco's daughter Maeve [94], who is in the WAAC's has just had a wonderful experience. She was walking on the country road hoping for a lift on the way to London with her friend Joan. They signalled a car that came along and it stopped and took them up and drove them the 40 miles to Windsor. The gray haired lady in it put Maeve to sit by her, and talked to her, asking about her work, throughout the journey, and at the end she gave them each a little medallion, engraved with M.R. on the one side and Good Luck on the other. It was Queen Mary, and she was on her way to the funeral of her son the Duke of Kent. [95]

Mrs Lilienfeld has been here this afternoon and we had such a happy time. After tea she helped me to gather the apples that are ripe and threatening to fall. Alas our wonderful crop is much reduced when they came to be gathered, by the ravages of earwigs and wasps. Then we came into the sitting room and she tried over her parts in Francesco's songs – such difficult intervals and very little time, though they are so melodious.

93 French: in return.

94 Correct spelling 'Maive'.

95 29 August 1942. Apparently Queen Mary had these medallions specially made for such occasions and her chauffeur was instructed to give lifts to service personnel.

Tuesday September 15, 1942

Yesterday I went at 3pm by Francesco's invitation to hear the rehearsal of his three part songs. On my way I left a note for the Blacks, telling them very regretfully that Noel would not be here for tea on the Saturday before his *"talk"*. He is taking part in a Fabian Conference on India, to be held that weekend at Oxford, making them promise to land him in Amersham on Sunday morning. I then went to Woolworth's to buy more black-out material. What was 1/11 last year is now 3/-: and this is marvellously cheap compared with what I was offered at Chesham for 5/11. Certainly that was more elegant, being thick Italian cloth: but neither would be useful for much after the War.
The rehearsal was well under way when I arrived at 3pm, and more people kept dropping in. We had arranged that I should get the tea, but it was all ready on the kitchen table, buttered and set out by Francesco. I am afraid I lost my head when I saw the room full of ladies and expecting them all to stay. All did stay, except the young Polish Countess [96]. She has just finished, he says, a beautiful portrait of him – *"all but the suit"*! He gave me 2/6 to buy delicacies and bread for he had sat for her till 10 o'clock forgetting that all shops now shut from 1pm – 2pm. So I went on my bicycle to forage for more. I felt very guilty when all the guests with one accord refused more than one piece and I left Francesco's 2/6 in the kitchen for him to find when I was gone.
Mrs Bunney helped me and poured out. She has been ill and is most unhappy. I hear from Georgia that Mr Bunney is such a Socialist that he refuses his two children more than a working class education.
The brilliant boy has been put to work at fifteen and is a perfect bore and the little girl, still at council school, has lost all interest in music, in which she was most promising and has been allowed to give it up, because the other children think it is *"sissy"* to play the piano [97].

96 Marie-louise Motesiczky.

97 Again Mabel has written inaccurate gossip about this family. These facts have now been checked with 'children' in question and shown to be incorrect, but they have given consent to the comments being published as the journal is one person's verbatim account. The Bunneys were members of the Society of Friends and all four of their children went to Quaker boarding schools, and went on to useful careers.

Monday September 21, 1942

I am writing before breakfast in bed at Bertie's. [98] I got off at 11.45pm on Saturday, after a very busy time and have been so tired ever since that I was quite glad to see the rain yesterday which kept us quietly in the sitting room. Thursday began at the dentists, where I had a huge back tooth pulled out. It had had a gold crown for just twenty years, put on by the Ilfracombe dentist shortly before we left. Since early spring it has been painful sometimes very painful, but I never suspected the abscess that Mr Wege found. I had promised to take a photograph at the Studio of Francesco and his three singing ladies, but didn't feel much like going after that! However the weather was so uncertain that I was afraid to put it off and this was fortunate, as all Friday afternoon I was making scones a cake and apple tarts. They were late in starting as Freda had not arrived and the rehearsal was begun by Mrs Burrows and Mrs Downer, singing Georgia's duet.

I wish the concert could have been kept sacred to one or the other of my friends. It was cruel to put Georgia's drawing room pieces – very pretty and attractive and Edwardian – to the test of comparison with Francesco's. It was nearly 4pm before I could take the photographs. We adjourned to the back garden and I used all the films remaining after the snaps of Mother's birthday. Then the rehearsal began again and this time I listened in Francesco's room to Georgia and Mrs Burrows. Mrs Black arrived meantime and joined the big group in the music room.

I got the tea with some spasmodic help from Mrs Burrows and we set it in the front garden, where we made a party of eight people with baby Janet and the dog, Tinker, who had come with Freda and stayed under the wing of his adored Francesco. Afterwards Georgia and Mrs Burrows (an enormous large stout prima donna-like figure who asked her to call her 'Pixie') went to sing over her songs for Mr Sloley whose housekeeper is away so that he can't leave the house. I had found to my horror that I had made a mistake in reading the last line of one of the German songs and translated 'Glück' [99] instead of 'Gluth' so that

98 An apartment overlooking the Thames at Richmond, Surrey.
99 German: luck.

I should have to alter the line which had already cost me a great deal of trouble. So with many apologies and after some pressure they left me to wash up for the eight people while the rehearsal began again in the Music Room and when I had finished I just departed as I was feeling ill. I had hoped to have the Friday free for preparations for Lucy, but half the morning went in altering and typing the two songs and taking them to Mrs Lilienfeld. I also had to go twice to the Martins [100], to arrange about the removal of the Cozy Stove [101]. When I got home it took me all my time to prepare our own dinner. Miss Barnes had volunteered to clean my bedroom with the vacuum, but met me with the news that there was no power in my room so that she had been obliged to go on with something else. I found when I looked that she had omitted to turn on the switch of the vacuum. It is a constant puzzle to me how these women run their own homes. I suppose she has a fairly average intelligence, but is helpless in the face of any event the least unusual and always rebukes me when I set to work to mend a flex, or the electric iron, or even to fix up a strip of wood that has come loose in the window frame – *"I should have thought it was a job for a workman – but you know best."* I certainly do!

Saturday was a beautiful sunny morning. I had a few jobs to do before I could leave the garden for the weekend. Lawrence during the week had appeared out of the blue and dug up all the potatoes and onions and laid them out to dry, promising to return in two days. When, as always, he failed to appear I got the barrow and with about five journeys landed the potatoes in a sack and the hay box in the garage. Unfortunately I did the same with the onions, but as I have learnt since that they must stay out three weeks above ground I carried them all back again and laid them out. The marrows, tomatoes and newly moved Buddleia all needed water, or I thought they did, but as it happens, they have had plenty during my absence from natural causes! I had time to spare at the Station and was sitting on a seat when Miss Robinson (our late Amersham friend who drove us to Welwyn) suddenly appeared. She had come for the day on business and stayed

100 Martin & Sons (Builders and Decorators) London Road West.
101 Her hall stove that she is lending to Ticciati.

talking till my train comes in. She is forty five and liable to be called up for War Work, so she volunteered and is doing clerical work for the Red Cross in London. She says the organisation is now so huge it is like a Government Department. Then at the first stop Francesco's young pupil, Connie Dupré, got in and we had a great talk about her Matric exam which had taken place the week previously on her one weeks' holiday. She told me that not only did Francesco teach her French, but Mr Black, the ex Senior Wrangler [102] coached her in Maths! She hopes to get a post as Librarian eventually, not liking business life. It was a quick train and I reached the flat comfortably about ten to one, an hour and five minutes after I left Amersham. [103] I took a Monthly Return ticket for 4/1 – much cheaper than the normal 6/9 and much dearer than the Workman's 1/7! Noel is still very seedy from his recurrent 'flu. He had spent Thursday in bed and says he had done no work for three weeks. It is good he has so much broadcasting to do as it is fantastically well paid and lets him go easy with his other work. I lay down in his bed after lunch and had a good rest while he went to fetch his watch which had been for three weeks at the repairer's. It is impossible now to get clocks repaired at all and watches are apt to stop work again an hour or two after they have been brought home. This time his watch was not ready, though the very hour had been specified in which he was to fetch it. We took [the] Tube straight to Kings Cross and then walked for about ¼ hour to the Eric Newton's house [104], crossing Kings Cross Road, which Noel had stoutly maintained to have no existence. After that the way lay up a steep hill, first through a mean Street and then round Percy Circus, into Lloyd Square and finally to the quiet backwater where they live. The neighbourhood had been much bombed and in one great empty space that had once been houses we saw a huge balloon on the ground. It was evidently just inflated and ready to soar for when we turned into our last *"Gardens"* it had risen and was floating almost above our heads. The front door was open, and my friend Mrs Burrows, alias Pixie, alias Carol Squires,

102 Top-scoring student with First Class Honours in the Mathematics Tripos degree at Cambridge.
103 Her Brother, Noel's, flat in Hampstead.
104 3 Cumberland Gardens, WC1.

standing there with Mary Evans, the beautiful calm teacher of dancing whom I had met at the Studio. The first thing we saw in the hall was Francesco's portrait facing all-incomers. The thing is a caricature and I felt it an outrage that all the visitors should think it to be his likeness, not knowing him as we do, – and what an utter lack of vanity the man must have to call it a beautiful portrait! I suppose it is in the most modern style, very rough in surface and full of blobs and black dashes. The Countess has painted him with his mouth open, and successfully wipes out all the nobility from his face, covering it, as I say, with spots and lodging it, neckless, upon a nest of yellow flannel where the collar and tie should be [105]. It makes me itch to get out my pencils and show Francesco what he really is – perhaps I will!

We got a warm welcome from the Newtons and to my joy he and Noel got together at once, as fellow journalists with many other interests in common. We were shepherded into a little back room where we each had a cup of tea and a few words with other people there, none of whom I knew till Georgia came in. Then we removed into the music room – front and back rooms thrown into one. Here were two pianos, an upright and a grand which did not figure together until the last item. Francesco's dances played by him and Georgia. We sat near the Lilienfelds (husband and mother) and the Countess, to whom I have now a lasting grudge for her portrait – she is such a dainty cap-a-pie [106] looking little person with a very *"I keep myself to myself"* manner – the last person you would expect to perpetrate such a coarse unpleasant daub. All the audience were a most interesting looking lot – many Jews – some Italians including Angel Grande, the violinist who was to have given a Concert with Francesco in London in July, but it didn't come off – his arm was bad at the time.

Francesco's boy came in just before it began – a really beautiful dark boy of nineteen, with a most attractive face, full of life and quite devoid of self consciousness. With him came his *"friend"* the very

105 Although Marie-louise Motesiczky's paintings are exhibited in major art galleries around the world, there appears to be no trace of this portrait of Francesco Ticciati.
106 Old English expression: from head to foot.

young (Austrian I think) pianist, who had played with him at the School Concert where he provided all the music. These two young things sat on the floor together. And so the Concert began. Noel said afterwards what a very interesting looking lot of people they were. He had a talk with Freda about the three love songs that she had sung in Hebrew and another chat with *"Stella"* our hostess – a few words with Francesco and a good long talk with Georgia about his talk in the Studio next Sunday. I was so very glad to find him at home and interested with my friends – a very new experience. Eric Newton is Art Critic for the Manchester Guardian and the house was very delightful – what we saw of it. There was a large *"picture"* of a horse facing us which intrigued Noel very much. We had made friends with young Oppenheimer who gave the Sunday talk during Georgia's illness, and he explained that the artist first made a bed of concrete and while it was wet built up the picture with bits of glass finally, he thinks, painting over the whole. The effect, and I imagine the purpose, was like a tessellated pavement. I think all the music went off very well. I enjoyed most Francesco's Prelude and Toccata, the two pieces with which he opened the second – his half – of the concert. Noel says he most enjoyed Mrs Lilienfeld's two German songs that I had translated. I think the two trios are far too difficult to be understood at one hearing. The three ladies were terribly nervous, being so anxious to do Francesco credit, but they went well. Then the audience broke up – they wanted us to stay with the special friends who remained, but I knew Noel was tired and it was also getting late for me to catch my bus to Richmond. As it was, we were half-way back to King's Cross before I found I had left my umbrella behind and I made Noel go on home while I returned to retrieve it. I got a bus easily, but as time went on I got more and more sick – partly I think out of hunger, for we had had nothing to eat at the Newton's, and we reached Richmond about 8.30pm – just before I should have had to disgrace myself. It was an hour after blackout time but fortunately a half moon saved it from total blackness and by dint of questioning I arrived safely outside Bertie's *"block of flats"*, where I saw her walking to and fro. She had been all the way down to the bus. It was a great mercy I met her, for when we went to the door of the flats we found it locked for the night. No one came when we rang, and Bertie had never thought of bringing her night key. At this point too a young messenger girl arrived on a bicycle, with a letter for the fourth floor. Bertie said we would have to toil up the fire escape iron staircase outside – till she thought of ringing at the door of her friend on the bottom floor, who quickly opened it and let us through her kitchen to the common hall. So ended Saturday and so ended the fine weather, for it has hardly stopped raining since. Only after tea there was a fine interval and we had a short walk across the beautiful gardens and along the tow path beside the Thames. The leaves are beginning to change and even to fall, and the old gardeners have already begun their ceaseless autumn task of sweeping them up. Today again Bertie made me stay in bed till well on in the afternoon, when we had tea and went to my bus. I was intending to get the train at 6.9pm of which Connie had told me, but I caught an earlier one about twenty to six, which carried me to my consternation to Chesham! But I caught a Windsor bus immediately as far as our station, where I picked up my bicycle and got home without serious rain, finding all very well and saw a little at Richmond of how the War affects housewives for here in the country we have our regular deliveries – the laundry comes once a fortnight and we give a weekly order to the grocer, over the telephone, but Bertie has to take her dirty linen herself to the laundry and carry back every ounce of grocery, meat and vegetables. Regulations are very strict about salvage and there is very little that may actually be thrown away. An old gentleman, a retired doctor, has left a printed paper of instructions at every house in the flats, and when the chutes are emptied he is there with a long stick to turn over the contents and rescue anything of any possible value. One thing puzzled me – Bertie is very fond of music and took all manner of certificates in her youth. Yet she begged me till I was ashamed and had to yield – to play on her piano which had not been tuned for two years and of which most of the notes rose no more after they had been struck! I had a queer experience coming home, for the train carried me on to Chesham (as I see I have already set down).

Wednesday September 30, 1942

Last day of September. We are in the thick of the black-out again and already it has to be in place by 7 o'clock. Yesterday was the last day for all Green Line 'buses – very awkward for people living on this road so far from the Station.

Last Sunday was Noel's talk at the Studio, and a most happy occasion. It was a beautiful sunny day sandwiched between very wet ones. He was taking the chair at a Conference on India, held in Oxford for the Fabian Society and had made them promise to bring him to Amersham in time for his talk on *"Gerrard Winstanley: The Light shining in Buckinghamshire."* [107] At my suggestion they brought him straight to the Studio. I made a macaroni cheese and joined him there about 12.30pm and soon after the Eric Newton's arrived from London and finally Francesco. Georgia had set the table in the Studio, but by this time it was so warm in the garden that we carried it out bodily on to the grass. Then ensued an amusing and I should think a very characteristic little interlude – Eric Newton insisting on placing the table in the right position relative to the house. A further argument followed as to who could sit facing the sun. The talk was very interesting – chiefly about the Conference from which Noel had just come. The Government had taken it seriously and sent down two spokesmen to uphold their policy. They had all (at this table) seen Noel advertised as taking the chair on this coming afternoon, and Georgia and Francesco had been perturbed and wondered should they ring me up about it. Lunch ended with Francesco's delicious coffee which none of us could praise highly enough. The Newtons went round to the Countess' house to restore the portrait and brought her on to the lecture. Francesco and I washed up as usual and then prepared the tea. By that time people were arriving and the room was almost full and we took our seats at the end of the sofa by the door. My other neighbour was that very nice looking woman whom I had last met on the morning when I found Georgia ill and made her bed and this friend

107 Leader of the 'True Levellers' (1609–1676). H.N. Brailsford spent years researching the Levellers and his book was published posthumously in 1961. H.N Brailsford, *The Levellers and the English Revolution,* (Cresset Press, London) 1961.

and I dusted the studio together. Noel spoke for about an hour to a most attentive audience and when he had finished there were interesting questions and comments from travelled people and from farmers. During tea Mr Sloley [108] held forth to his neighbour about the good rule of the British in India particularly in the matter of making dams, and at last Noel broke in and put the whole thing in another light by remarking that we charge 10% for the use of them [109].

On Monday Mrs Pearce had asked me to write an account of the talk which I promised to do if she would add any necessary frills. This perturbed me all through Monday when I was expecting the Blacks to tea.

Tuesday was the morning when the hall stove was called for and transported to the Studio by one of the Martins. When I arrived at three for my lesson he was still working at it and made a very good job. Then we all helped him to move the heavy furniture so that the piano could be next [to] the stove. Francesco's joy in this acquisition was quite pathetic – *"Che Bellezza!"* [110], he exclaimed. I was to have tea with Georgia on Saturday, but she rang me up to say Francesco's boy, Niso, had arrived for the weekend and as he himself would be absent all day she was taking him to the theatre and would I come a little later than five, but I went in time to get our tea ready and had it waiting out in the sun at the front. Niso is a most delightful boy – brilliantly clever and yet absolutely free from self-consciousness. We were soon at home together, and talking freely over tea. *"Che angelo!"* [111]

Thursday October 8, 1942

Mrs Lilienfeld (Kendra) came to take me out mushrooming yesterday. It was a queer hot steamy day, like the inside of a dirty greenhouse. The old man of the woods, the only bearded inhabitant of Amersham, whose appearance has not changed by one hair, nor I should think, has

108 It is not clear which Mr Sloley this is, Father or Son. The Father was born in Calcutta and the son had worked for the Incian Education Service.

109 Noel was also very knowledgeable on Indian affairs. He was an executive member of the Indian League, a writer on Indian affairs and who had worked with Ghandi and Nehru on Indian politics.

110 Italian: *what a beauty.*

111 Italian: *what an angel.*

he ever washed himself since we came to live in Little Elms – came over the hill while we were there, with a bulging bag. He had been collecting all morning and afternoon and sells them to the shops.

On Sunday Niso came alone to tea. I hadn't wanted to take him away from his father, but Francesco wished him to come, as he himself had had no time to practise since his arrival on Friday morning. I don't think he was a bit shy and talked very freely of his teaching and his practising under difficulties. He had been getting up at 5.30am, shutting himself in the music room and playing the 'cello (the school cello) with muted strings, because the headmaster refused to allow him time for practise. After tea he apologized for having eaten so much, *"for I'm not a schoolboy now!"*. He was immensely interested in the cuckoo clock, its bellows, and the interval of its cuck. Miss Holmes and Miss Isaacs came in to thank me for planting two rows of Russian Kale in their absence the previous morning, so Niso played to us all. First the setting of *"Nature I Loved and after Nature, Art"*. A most effective little quatrain of music, which he says is much more effective as he wrote it for three women's voices (it seems to run in the family). Then four little pieces written for his pupils of about twelve years of age; most charming and varied and far too difficult I think unless they are young Mozarts, and finally a solemn piece rather in the style of Bach. He has only been able to study music for the last four years and has never had a lesson. In his short life he has had a time of bitter poverty (this must have been just before his parents separated), but now he is keeping himself and has the prospect of Oxford after the War. But he wants to be a Conductor and that he says is what Francesco advises.

I have just brought in a tremendous harvest of green tomatoes and alas have only 1lb of sugar, a gift from Lucy, towards preserving them. Tomorrow Miss Barnes will cut up the French beans I have just gathered and we will lay them down in salt. Last year I had two big crocks full, and they stood us in very good stead in emergencies.

Thursday October 15, 1942

On Monday I went to town to the Osteopathic Clinic, which has cured Francesco's longstanding trouble with his arm. I have to leave this house at ten to seven which will very soon be within the blackout time, and there is a mile and a half, mostly uphill to the Station. On Monday it was fine, but bitterly cold. Very beautiful with white mist lying in the Misbourne Valley and the sun just rising behind the woods in a glory of pink clouds. But I grew colder and colder as I went, partly I think out of apprehension for I had a great dread of any errand. When I reached the Station my hands were so numb that after many attempts I was obliged to ask the ticket girl to open my purse! I was taking Noel a big bunch of Michaelmas daisies and two small ones of rosebuds and *"tinies"* and also his dressing gown that we are giving him for Christmas. He made me wear it in front of the electric fire in his bedroom where we had breakfast, and I thawed out under the influence of hot coffee. He was not at all well. I had unfortunately arrived after his night of fire watching, when he could have stayed later in bed, and on the Sunday afternoon he had taken part in a most realistic Fire Exercise, conducted by Wardens, crawling under obstacles and extinguishing fires through dense smoke. I found the Clinic easily at Buckingham Gate. The man who examined me was named Webster Jones and turned out most strangely to know Amersham well. His wife and children were evacuated to Little Elms and later to Mrs Barretts where he joined them at weekends and Mr Black had taught him Maths. I am to go up twice a week for the present. Paying is left to the patients' will and conscience and mine it appears work on the same lines as Francesco's! 10/- for the consultation and 5/- a time for treatment, unless it should be very prolonged, when I shall have to make a reduction. I had my Italian lesson next day. It cheered me up for I was feeling very depressed. The examination had left me with a lot of pain and Mr Webster Jones had seemed doubtful whether I should be able to stand the treatment, but now (Friday) I have got home after a most hopeful séance [112]. Certainly it hurt me

112 Meaning: session.

pretty badly both in the arm and the spine, but I felt relief as soon as I got off the operating sofa. He treated me on a very creaky couch and he said *"This couch is doing all the groaning that you ought to be doing"*. It was a glorious sunny day and I sat in the Gardens looking on Buckingham Palace, watching the relief of the Guard – shorn of all its spectacular glamour since the men were all in Khaki. Then I set out to walk on the left of the river towards the towers of Westminster, and found myself at St. James' Palace. From there I came to the National Gallery, where I spent about an hour, looking at the War Artists' Exhibition. I saw again Muirhead's wonderful St. Bride's and Ludgate Hill after the Blitz. Another of his struck me particularly – a torpedoed Oil Tanker – and again a most impressive Minelaying at Sea. It is strange how these three stood out from all the other pictures and I went straight to them before I knew the artist's name. St. Bride's carries its signature in every line, but the other two have a technique that I have not seen before in Muirhead's work. Still walking, malgré moi [113], I came up Charing Cross Road, and finally got a thirteen bus in Piccadilly Circus, which landed me at Finchley Road Station in comfortable time for my 1.39pm train (I forgot to mention the most lifelike bust of M. Maesky by Epstein, which faces one in one of the rooms – a marvellous piece of work.) Now to return to the Music Studio. Mrs Black came in after my lesson and talked for half an hour, giving us the most heart rending revelations about the state of the board schools. Owing partly to the influx of evacuee children and partly to the calling up of teachers, the classes are of not less than fifty. The teachers warned her before she began that they made no attempt to teach anything and were content if they could keep order. This is only done by caning and the children will neither learn nor behave themselves under any other stimulus. She told me one sad story to confirm this. She was walking along one of the passages and raised her arm to ward off one of the sandbags which threatened to fall on her.

113 French: *in spite of myself.*

A good little boy who was innocently coming toward her shrank away and put up his arm to shield himself from the blow that he thought was coming. Learning associated with pain.

[There is an inserted scrap of paper here. It says, *"Mr Churchill said in Parliament that this Battle of Egypt is one of the major victories of English history, and all the Church Bells are to ring on Sunday morning."*]

Thursday October 22, 1942

[Strange handwriting]

I shan't see Noel tomorrow. He is going to Oxford today to take part in a debate at the Oxford Union and won't be home till Friday afternoon. But Mrs Pollak his refugee will get me breakfast. All round Victoria one sees none but Polish soldiers, both men and women. They are very like ourselves – one would never take them to be foreigners. I was interested to see a nearly built aeroplane (without its wings) being conveyed through the streets on a lorry. It was of such great length that it was impossible to turn it in an ordinary space and it had to be conveyed by devious ways – a hair-raising task for the driver. Another strange sight was a huge dump of coal and anthracite that is being accumulated in a great empty space, half way down Baker Street. It is on the site of Druce's shop [114] which was completely bombed out in the Blitz.

Monday November 9, 1942

[In pencil in strange writing, probably because of the strapping]

I have been going to the Clinic for four weeks, twice a week. I think I am definitely beginning to yield to treatment. They concentrated at first on the shoulder, where they said the muscles were in a dreadful mess. Now it is bound up with strips of elastoplast, and I am to rest it while they turn their attention to the spine and to the muscles of the leg, which has become half an inch shorter than the other. The manipulation and massage hurt me very much, but now I know they

114 Druce & Co., Furniture Galleries and Showrooms, 56, 58, 68 and 69, Baker Street, London.

are doing me good. The first three weeks were a progressive nightmare, as the mornings grew darker. The last time I started in almost total darkness, after a night when I woke nearly every hour for fear of not waking at six. I found I could not balance on my bicycle in the dark and fell off twice. After this Noel insisted on paying my fares by a Christian [?] train [115] – the cheapest return is now 4/9. I make sandwiches, and eat them generally near Birdcage Walk beside the water and in the company of the tamest sparrows pigeons and waterfowl. Today a sparrow ate out of my hand!

Yesterday was Frida Danziger's recital at S[tudio]. Francisco playing her accompaniments throughout, and entirely from memory. The Studio was almost full, and nearly all were manifest Jews. It was a very well balanced and varied programme, beginning with old Italian songs, such as Scarlatti and Marcello, a group of songs in English and finally five or six sung in German of which the most beautiful I think was Gretchen at the Spinning Wheel. [116] Francesco's accompaniment was so exquisite.

(On Thursday Bertie met me at 11.45am outside Gossinge's for lunch) [117]. It was followed by the funniest tea party, Mrs Gordon West, Eileen (who suggested she should join the Italian lessons) were at one end with old Miss Violet Defries (who told Georgia that she came of the Defries's of Shoreditch) and Frida Dancyger. Then came Hendra Lilienfeld, Francesco, myself round the corner, and Georgia pouring out. The conversation mostly came from the far end, for Frida was garrulous with the glow of her success, and did not say one unkind or grumbling word. She was talking about a Recital she had given long ago in the Wigmore Hall, for which she sold nearly 200 tickets beforehand, so she felt justified in buying herself the most beautiful frock she had ever had, and someone presented her with stockings the exact shade, costing I think 14/6. Thus arrayed, she felt no nervousness

115 It is unclear what she means by this, but in September 1942 all Green Line buses were withdrawn to save fuel and rubber, and fares were increased to discourage all but essential travel.

116 Meine Ruh ist hin by Franz Schubert.

117 Department store, Buckingham Palace Road. closed 1968.

when she came to sing. (I once asked Francesco why she didn't get engagements like Mrs Lilienfeld, and he said it was because of her manner, and that nobody likes her until they know her very well – she seems so hard). This started Eileen and Mrs Gordon West on the subject of clothes and they agreed that quite nice frocks could be had in Marshall's inexpensive department for six or eight guineas. Eileen also treated the table to a detailed account of the behaviour of a gold-crowned tooth, and her fears for its future. We sat pretty quiet at our end! Before the Concert Mrs West was telling me what a pity it was that Noel had not read over his lecture beforehand, and cut out a lot of it. She herself had done a lot of public speaking and always followed this plan. When I told this colloquy to Georgia and Francesco, he told us that after one of his recitals she assured him that she herself played two of the pieces, but she played them with more soul!

Sunday November 15, 1942

Mr Churchill said in Parliament that this Battle of Egypt is one of the major victories of English history, and all the Church Bells are to ring on Sunday morning [118]. We began with Church Bells from Westminster, Edinburgh, Llandaff and Armagh, and then because two years ago last night the Germans bombed Coventry and destroyed a great part of the City, we ended with chimes from Coventry Cathedral where only the bell tower is still standing and they played *"O God our help in ages past."*

Monday November 23, 1942

Noel was so sorry to go back to town by the 2.30pm train. The winter sunshine was so beautiful and he would have liked to go with me to Francesco's Recital at the Tory Uncle's studio. He had been asked to take the chair at a meeting of German refugees, to discuss plans for Germany after the War. He told me he had just had an important little success in this connection, having induced the two parties of German

118 El Alamein. This was the first time church bells were rung since June 1940, and the sound of the main peals were broadcast. Since the invasion threat of 1940 church bells had been silenced only to be rung in the event of an imminent invasion.

Communists and Socialists to be reconciled and work together for the common cause. And hereby hangs a rather unpleasant tale. I have often recorded my resolve never again to argue or even discuss anything with Miss Barnes, for that way lies the only hope of peace. She questioned me closely about Noel's meeting and I told her it was a Meeting of German refugees to discuss how they could best build a new Germany after the War. *"O"*, she said, *"if they think they are going to have a hand in it they will find they are mistaken – we and the Russians will take good care of that. There's going to be an Army of Occupation in Germany for years and years after the War."* When I could get a word in, which was not soon, I asked if she remembered when Stalin stated his War aims. He said he had no intention of interfering in the internal government of Germany or any other European country once peace had been made. *"He didn't"* said Miss Barnes. It was so rude, that I exclaimed *"Miss Barnes, I don't think you can know how rude you are."* She wasn't either abashed or vexed, but continued in a worse strain than before, to assure me that Stalin is urging his armies to press on into Germany and kill every German they meet there … I asked how she could look forward to a new Europe founded on hate; but one might as well reason with the Falls of Lodore [119]. Her last retort is that I can't be all British, and I don't love my country – this was because I corrected her when she asserted that England had never persecuted the Jews. She seems to think that the test of patriotism is that one should hate every other nation. Apparently the BBC have the same mental outlook, for this week Eric Newton asked them why they hadn't been engaging Francesco, and they replied [that] Of course they would be glad to have him only they were not satisfied about his nationalization!

Miss Barnes went shopping in Aylesbury on Tuesday, so we had Francesco here for lunch and tea and my lesson, and he played to Mother for nearly an hour, his own Prelude, by my request, a Beethoven Sonata, a lot of Scarlatii. Then he said there was something else he wanted to play – I thought it was his own, but it was César

119 A waterfall in Cumbria.

Franck. He told me more about himself than he had ever done before – of the unhappy childhood, shadowed by the threat of hell – a threat which always returns, in spite of reason, when he is unwell or depressed, as in the attack of 'flu in the summer. It was darkened too by the doctrine that all pleasure is sinful, and this had in the end the effect of making him deceive. Finally there was the threat of military service, held over him always if he complained of any discomfort or asked for any luxury. Finally there was the cruelty to animals and to birds, which he saw all around him and this alone he says would prevent him every going back to live in Italy, unless, as I suggested, as a missionary …
I asked him about the recital of his compositions, which was to have taken place this month. It is all off because Frida has again turned nasty. Francesco says he has endured her temper for twenty years and has always been the one to bear the olive branch. But at last he feels he has had enough, and is going to leave her to come round of herself. He says it has taken him twenty years to overcome his own bad temper! When he came to England his one wish was to be left alone for his work and to leave everyone else alone, but England has changed all that. This was good hearing.

Monday December 28, 1942

I am in bed in the Music Room at the Studio – a beautiful and incredible circumstance! The Clinic hasn't been doing me any good lately. I suppose it is true as they say, that I am not strong enough to profit by the treatment. A fortnight before my final visit I was delivered over to two new practitioners – young men who had been recruited to the staff. The BMA will still not countenance the Osteopath – though' individual doctors are often friendly and the staff are being called up to ordinary army duties in which their special knowledge and training are of no use. These two talked all the time – shop mostly – over my prostrate form. One was Irish, but he was quite merciless and seemed to look upon me as an inanimate object. I told him he was hurting me very badly, and he neither ceased nor even replied – and again when he pulled my neck out of its socket (if it has one) and jerked it back again – I exclaimed *"I thought that would have broken my spine"*, but I got no reply. I was so nervy when I got back that I fell off trying to mount my bicycle and on the Monday I was in such continuous pain that I made two resolves – to miss my treatment for that day, and to ask as a favour that I might never again be treated by the Irishman. But alas when I arrived on the Thursday I seemed to be the only patient – there was no sign of my friend Mr Webster Jones nor of the very nice woman almoness [120]. There was nothing to be done but make the best of the Irishman who came forward to meet me. So I began about Ireland and told him of my Dublin ancestors. When he at once became a kind and humane human being. We had much talk about Dublin. He asked me what I thought about Eire's attitude in the War and I replied I am afraid I am rather ashamed of her! [121] To which he answered *"They are the only Nation who have managed to keep sane when all the rest are mad."* Certainly they have pulled it off so far, but as Noel says they are not yet out of the wood! He told me at my request, when he was going to hurt me, and we parted very good friends. In fact he asked me to make it convenient, if I could, to come at one o'clock a week from then. That proved to be my last treatment, for he told me then not to come again until or unless I had had a holiday – and conversely, if I had a holiday I should need no more treatment, *"You need it very badly and nothing will take the place of it"*. He also told me to take Bilson's Nerve Food, which I was lucky enough to find in Boots in Buckingham Palace Road. He wanted me to go to Dublin and wander on the hills. Noel came on Thursday and on Friday. I let Miss Barnes out for the day and Francesco came for lunch and tea. Mother was on the sofa, very happy, and Francesco played for us – an early Beethoven and then the Appassionata. Noel was distressed about me, and asked me to go to Mrs Barrett for a week when I leave here tomorrow, and he will pay for it. I have been in bed ever since I came, though yesterday I moved into Francesco's room – very warm with the cozy stove from our hall and we read Italian together. The first evening Mrs Black came in after supper and we had a most interesting and entertaining time. She has a

120 An almoner is an archaic term for a social worker, Mr Webster Jones assistant.

121 Eire was neutral during the war.

mind that moves with lightening quickness. The two little boys, John and Leo eleven and ten are wonder children in writing and music. John gave Georgia for Christmas a poem about a Roman Arch, which wouldn't have disgraced a boy of twenty, except for the two last lines – and Leo a Minuet written and harmonized by himself. Mrs Black told us of the days when she first left college, when she more or less toured South Wales as an unpaid speaker for the ILP [122]. Amongst other striking things she remarked that we spend our time doing little things and talking about big ones.

I am sleeping on Georgia's divan with two grand pianos on my right, and Georgia's stretcher against the far wall. Last night a gale sprung up and we woke to find a hard frost and a sprinkling of snow. This morning Francesco had a girl pupil from London, at eleven o'clock. She began with single notes – then arpeggios – ending with a very finely played piece of Schubert's. Her name is Richenda May. The first Richenda I have met in the flesh. She is of course of Quaker origin. She went with us afterwards to see the Crib at Elangeni [123], that Angelo Crovo, Irma Colenso's husband, has made for their little evacuees (triplets born just before the war, to the woman who was once engaged to their brother). It was in a window embrasure in the big music room, shut off by wooden gates. Mary was kneeling on the left, almost lifesize with a very quiet worshipping face and attitude – the baby at her feet was rather disproportionately small (perhaps Mr Crovo couldn't get any more papier maché). To my mind the baby's face spoilt the group, as it was quite colourless and it looked like a dead child. On the right was a very realistic heap of sheep skin in place of the cow and ass, and a small picture behind represented the journey of the three wise men. Then they took us up to see the three children. We found them alone in their cribs, just awaking from a siesta. They are very attractive little girls, full of life, with shining dark eyes and beautiful little bodies, indistinguishable one from the other. Their parents were married sixteen years before they arrived.

122 Independent Labour Party.
123 A large house in Chestnut Lane, Amersham. Now the site of a school of the same name.

Tuesday 29 December, 1942

Inserted in the diary is an unfinished letter she was writing to her Mother from the Music Studio.

Darling Mother,

I wonder how you are this lovely sunny morning—and did Susie [124] come to you first thing to give you her little hand on the bed? Now I imagine Mrs Coleman is doing your fire. I am so happy and already much better. My shoulder is much easier. We had tea when I arrived and then Georgia made me get into my dressing gown. I had my bath at that point too, so as not to interfere with the others. Georgia spent a long time getting supper. I don't think it was anything extra for me but it was more like dinner – a delicious cheese and egg dish, followed by stewed apple and milk pudding. Meantime Francesco sat and talked to me. It is very hard for him not to feel discouraged, getting so little recognition. Sometimes he feels he never wants to play again. He says he feels like a performing animal set up on a music stool for people to applaud. (He is now doing the most marvellous arpeggios in his own room.) After supper Mrs Black came in – you remember she is the wife of Noel's friend who was on the Spanish Committee – and we had a most entertaining hour. She is a most attractive and very witty woman with a brain that works at lightning speed. She has been a great admirer of Noel's writing from the time she left College. They have two wonderful boys of eleven and ten. I think I have told you about them. For Christmas the elder one sent Georgia a poem about an old Roman gateway, and the younger a Minuet composed and written by himself. We went to bed after she had gone. Francesco got me a hot bottle! Georgia does the sitting room fire and he does the kitchen and his own room fires, and all the washing up, and gets the breakfast. I am going to have the house to myself. Georgia was rung up in the middle of tea by a friend with whom she had promised to have tea and had forgotten all about it. So she is going round to have coffee at 11am, and Francesco has gone to give a French lesson to the little Bunney girl.

124 Mabel's dog.

They won't let me do the least thing, except that I may mend a pair of Francesco's socks and sew some buttons on! I think I worry far too much over unimportant things. They have lost their very good temporary maid and have no prospect of another, and [have] a person trying to be an invalid staying with them, but the whole atmosphere is so calm and happy. You can imagine how I want to group and clean the house and cook the dinner while they are both out, but I did unfortunately promise not to and it wouldn't be fair ...

Friday 1 January, 1943

c/o Mrs Barrett.

On Wednesday evening Connie came in at eight o'clock to thank me for Henry Pooley's [125] letter, with advice as to how she should set about obtaining the BSc. She is anxious to get out of the Insurance Brokers, where she has been working for two years and to get into an atmosphere not entirely obsessed by money. She had a notion she would like to be associated with astronomy and wrote to Dr Jeans [126] for advice on obtaining a librarian's or similar post in the Observatory. He told her she would need the BSc degree. She wrote also to the Associated Body of Librarians (or some such title) and on Wednesday their reply arrived. They said, in a printed circular, that librarians were usually trained from young people of 17–19 (Connie is 21). They must have spent one year in some library before they take the first examination and there are three to follow, and without this training their prospects of obtaining work would be remote. She and Francesco both seemed to give up hope when they read this letter, though Georgia was sure that there were other means of approach to the profession. The letter seemed to stir up all the bitterness of Francesco's vain search for employment. In spite of his title of Doctor of Music of London University, no college or even school will take him on their staff because he is not vouched for by the Royal Academy. Connie left about ten, and when Francesco came back after seeing her through the darkest part of the road, we sat round the fire till 12.15am talking over past and futures. He told us that the blind pianist, Keith Burrows, is given smaller fees for Recitals, simply because he is blind. Francesco is in the deepest depression about his prospects. He has had little but very unfriendly criticism for his recitals and this has so discouraged him that he sits down to the piano either very morose and discouraged or else truculent, and either mood is fatal to his playing. I tried to get at the reason for these bad notices (he says he feels like a performing animal). He finally explained that the musicians of Britain, which term includes the important critics, seem to be a closed body and will not countenance any artist who has not passed through the mill. (Like the Librarians and like the British Medical Association). He told us of two separate occasions when a critic of one of the big London dailies had come up to him after a recital, full of joy and praise and enthusiasm – and next day a most scathing criticism of his performance appeared over the signature of this

125 Great nephew of Clara Brailsford and second cousin of Mabel.
126 James Hopwood Jeans, Cambridge.

same critic. We discussed a removal to some other country. *"Why shouldn't we all emigrate?"* Francesco asked and I said I didn't want to live out of England. I suggested a return to Italy after the war, but his face clouded over and he exclaimed, *"Never! Italy is the Gate of Hell!"* Switzerland he rejected as an unmusical country and Germany of course as antagonistic in thought and feeling. (I begin to understand the Italian hatred of their German neighbours, now that I am studying *"Italia di Domani"*) [127] America he hates and would he says starve if he went to S.America as Busoni did in his youth. He was Professor of Music in Buenos Aires University and was paid by a percentage on each pupil, but never attracted a greater number than four. I don't know how he can be so brave and so sunny and so full of fear and go on working so hard to perfect his playing. His life seems to have been a series of blows and disappointments from the beginning. There were two brothers and a sister older than he: he was the youngest by ten years so that he had he says five parents all trying to keep him in order, instead of the normal two. They wished him to become a monk and gave him for mental pabulum, the Lives of the Saints. He still remembers the Life of the Beata Somebody which his Mother gave him to read as a small boy, and he flung it with all his force across the room. His says his childhood was so unhappy that he determined never to have a child – and Maeve and Niso are *"his two sins"*. Whereas Giorgia remarked that she hoped he had never committed any worse sins than those two delightful children. I said I am sure you saw to it that their childhood was very happy and he replied, very surprisingly to me, *"Ours was the most gloomy household you could imagine and after Frida came into it, it was gloomier still."* (When Niso came to see us he said he had called on his way to pay his respects at Flint House, but *"Frida was fortunately lying down"*) Frida told Georgia that Niso was a most impertinent little boy. When she was living with them, their servant left and Niso said *"I am sorry you are going, Jane, you are the one ray of sunshine in this house."* – My wish for Frida, if it was a wish, has come to pass and she has quarrelled again with Francesco, on his birthday, and never comes near the Studio – She asked him how he was going to spend Christmas and when he said he was coming to us she asked were we his oldest friends? *"They are not my oldest friends,"* he replied, *"very uneasily, but perhaps they are nicer than those who are!"*

127 L'Italia di domain, Pentade (Penguin, 1942).

I didn't think I should sleep after this long late talk, but I fell asleep instantly and never woke till 8.30am, when I heard Francesco raking out the boiler fire. He brought the breakfast in the merriest frame of mind, and while he was still harking back to his early life, he kept us in fits of laughter with stories of the strange characters he knew as a young man in Rome, in the musical profession. I had no idea he is, as Georgia says, a born actor and we could see the conductor striding about the room beating his hands together in despair while the recalcitrant pianist leans back in his chair, arms folded and an angelic smile on his face holding out silently for 5/- a night increase in salary, to equal that of the first violin *"or else I leave Rome"*.

The old year has gone out in an Olla Podrida [128] of weather. The first night at the Studio a wild gale sprang up, the windows rattled and objects were flung on the floor. We woke to find a hard frost and ice on the roads. The third night snow fell fairly heavily, but before we got up a thaw had set in and I was able to ride home on my heavily laden bicycle. Francesco made us all a stirrup cup of his delicious coffee, meantime setting a chair for me in the kitchen and switching our three days' discussion from his own past and prospects to mine. All these past months I have been troubled because when I asked him if he had read any of my writing, he said Yes, he had read two chapters of Susanna – and there stopped. Ever since I have wondered what there was in Susanna that could bore him – or was it that the life in that Leicestershire vicarage was so remote from his interest that it was impossible for him to envisage it. And it hurt me rather, for my books are me – the best part of me. But now he gave me the explanation. *"I read two chapters of one of your books, he said, but I couldn't read any more. I was so furious to know that you could do such work and were not doing it."* and so we passed on to a discussion that seemed to cover the whole field of service for the community – and of the duty of the State to see that everyone has leisure and opportunity to develop the best that is in him. And meantime the kettle was cold.

Noel had a strange most strange dream during the Christmas week. His old French teacher M. Durdac, at Dundee High School, was thrashing his shoulders with a cane and he bore it without protest, for he knew that for every stroke one of their taxes was remitted to the Indian peasants …. Francesco also had a dream that he was showing one of his compositions to his friend Victor Grove and he told him to re-write the five last movements in the style of Scarlatti.

128 Spanish stew. (Literal translation: rotten pot).

Thursday 7 January, 1943

Welwyn Garden City

I travelled here yesterday from Kings Cross, very much interested in my fellow travellers, two boys going to Cambridge, the first with a violin and *"Evolution"* Julian Huxley's new book, and the other with a folio of architectural drawings which he studied till he went to sleep. To [join] us almost at the last moment entered a WAAF, very stout and considerably made up, though quite young. She took the remaining corner, exclaiming *"What a rush!"* to the world at large. Little by little, being blessed with a glad eye which she exercised first upon the two Tommies who were leaning up against our window in the corridor, she got into a lively conversation with the architectural boy (the other by this time was consuming sandwiches of an incredible thickness.) We learnt that she had been traveling since 7.30pm the evening before, from South Wales – it was not 12.20pm. That she was returning to Hatfield from ten days embarkation leave and didn't of course know where she was being sent *"I don't want to go abroad,"* she said, *"and I didn't want to be in this at all. I never thought they would take me, as I was a private secretary."* She faded from our view at Hatfield Station, with repeated cheerio's to the architectural student, and *"All the best"* from him. I am sitting now in Lucy's little kitchen, beside the anthracite boiler fire. I didn't want her to light the drawing room fire, because of the fuel saving order, from which I have been suffering so severely at Mrs Barrett's. Lucy has gone out to do some of her War Savings Collecting in the neighbourhood. We have come back from a very wonderful war film *"In Which We Serve"* written and produced by Noel Coward who also acted the chief part. It is entirely concerned with the life (and death) of the Navy, afloat and ashore – on an HMS Destroyer Torrin – and clinging to a raft in the middle of the sea. It was banned for some time in America, because two of the sailors say *"Damn"*. I suppose these words have been deleted from the transatlantic edition, and it is now acclaimed as the picture of the year. Again, as in Mrs Miniver, we saw a chapter in the great epic of the Dunkirk Evacuation and we saw the blitz upon the houses of women and children. It was strange that my abiding reaction to this picture is wonder that Clare [129] can banish herself from this country and of the pride that burnt in me all through the autumn of 1940 that I am an Englishwoman, however unworthy. At the back of my mind I am going over and over the talk I had with Francesco

129 Clare Leighton, Noel's partner, went to live in America at the end of 1938.

before my last lesson on Tuesday and wondering where is to be found the way out. He says he has never earned enough to keep a home together and is far happier now that he can pay his way with one room to himself.
I asked him why he should not get together a quartette and go about the country. He said he is a martinet in his own profession and will have music as he thinks it ought to be, and where was he to find three artists with the same artistic conscience. He says they won't stand being corrected and quarrels always result, as in his last concert about a year ago with the violinist Angel Grande. He wished to alter a score and as Francesco thought this immoral, there was a first class row. In the end Francesco climbed down and they played the emendation at the concert. Then he said if he got together a quartette they would have to live near each other and make it their life work.

The Sunday before the blind pianist and his wife gave a concert, and I told Francesco I had not enjoyed it at all. Partly, I definitely dislike Schumann's Carnaval, all except the little mounting passage that recurs in Papillons. Francesco said he had never been able to learn it! Mr Burrows also played the whole book of Grieg that Mabel Esplin [130] and I played those Easter holidays in Blairgowrie [131] including the Watchman's Song and quoting Mrs Gordon West, I said we schoolgirls played it with more soul!! Francesco said he liked the little Elfentanz, and I said Yes, but he should have made it far more sprightly and fairy-like. But I said I feel a beast to criticize a blind man's playing … Francesco's joy seems still to grow in the stove that we gave him. He says it is a veritable benedicio [sic] di Dio.

Inserted in the diary was this letter, not sent, to Lucy Knowles, her cousin.

Dearest Lucy, at Malvern, [132] Amersham.

I am so sorry, but seeing the weather today. I think it is only sensible to give up the idea of coming to you. We have had snow and the sky is full of it. If I came and couldn't come home, it would be a disaster for both of us, and the fuel question is so acute, that I feel as if that alone was a sufficient reason. You know the doctor at the Clinic told me ten days would make a new person of me, when he knew my position, he didn't

130 Mabel's school friend. Both Mabels were boarding at Wintersdorf School, Trafalgar Road, Birkdale Lancs in 1891.

131 Where Mabel was living with her parents at that time.

132 Mrs Barrett's house.

suggest my taking longer, only Noel wouldn't hear of my giving up the weekend with you. Will you let me come in the Spring, if Miss Barnes will? If it hadn't been for the cold, Mrs Barrett's would have been an ideal refuge. I got practically well at Mrs Pearce's sleeping in the big room with the Cozy stove and having a very hot bath in a very warm bathroom. I had almost forgotten my various pains when I came here. But alas this bedroom is an ice house with no provision for heating it. I went to bed as soon as I arrived, but found I couldn't see either to read or to write. It is a very poor light shining straight into one's eyes. I washed piecemeal in a very cold bathroom and then lay in bed and shivered with my eyes shut. Next day I brought my reading lamp from home, and fixed it by the bed, so that I am right for light, but since I have got chilled to the bone two or three times, my shoulder has been far worse than ever it was even at first. Today Mrs Barrett brought me my breakfast a little earlier, and carried in the little electric heater on a long flex, from her father's room. So I started the day comparatively warm. It isn't her fault. She is just as kind and good as she could possibly be, but she doesn't know how she can manage with her coal allowance of 5cwt a month. It seems to me a very stupid arrangement to have a second kitchener [133] in the scullery and do all her cooking on that, while she has a roaring fire in the kitchen for the old gentleman to sit by, and neither of them heats the water. I am trying to spare the sitting room fire and stay in bed when I would far rather be up. Yesterday I sat by it in my big coat and a hot bottle to my feet. In spite of the pain being worse, I believe I myself am quite well again. I judge this, for I am beginning once more to make plans so that I can get some time for writing. If only Miss Barnes would leave me alone and in peace for any stretch of time, I should have some hope, but she doesn't know the meaning of the word study. How could she? And thinks I can go back to it quite happily after innumerable interruptions. I know I came at last to the conclusion that it was better not to try, for the continual disappointments got on my nerves so badly. Dear Lucy I know you don't mind my grumbles. I am very conscious that I am extraordinary lucky to have her – poor Mrs Pearce is once more entirely without help, but Dr Ticciati does all the washing up and two fires and makes his own bed and gets tea and breakfast.

[End of inserted letter]

133 Cooker.

Wednesday 13 January, 1943

This letter was never sent to Lucy, for the snow and frost vanished in a night, and I duly went to Welwyn on the Thursday. Snow and frost came back next day, joined to a bitter north east wind. Lucy has been sitting in her very comfortless kitchen before the boiler fire, reserving the fire in her pretty sitting room for two days a week. We woke on Sunday morning to find the frost gone and a drizzle falling, but it had left it's legacy, underfoot in a sheet of ice, which made our journey to the station very slow and perilous. There was a fairly heavy fog and my train for London which should have left Welwyn at 11.29am, did not arrive till 12 noon. When it was carrying the passengers due to arrive at 11.15am as well. The corridor was crowded and I was very lucky to get what seemed to be the only seat in the train. We reached Kings Cross at 12.50pm leaving me ten minutes instead of an hour to catch my train at Baker Street which by some miracle which I don't yet understand I managed to do! The fog was thick at Amersham. Georgia was hoping that her two friends Mr & Mrs Kenning would have a great influence on Francesco. They have been for three years in the U.S. preaching and lecturing a vague sort of transcendentalism. The Studio was almost full and sixteen stayed to tea in Francesco's room. Mr Kenning who is a parson of the Church of England gave an address which could in part have come from a Methodist pulpit but he differed in preaching transmigration (is that the right word?). He said with dogmatism that the reason for our weltschmerz (he didn't use that expression) [134] was that our race had once known complete happiness and harmony with God and that we were homesick for a home we had once known – just as we should most certainly find it again. When questions were invited, Mr Milburn, who generally plays the role of der Geist der stets verneint [135] rose and for once gave a voice to what at any rate all the thinking audience had been questioning. He asked what date could be assigned to this Garden of Eden state and at what stage of our evolution had it been engaged? Then he went on to give what he called the acknowledged scientific explanation for this universal belief – there had been a stage, not in racial but in every individual life, when we were perfectly safe and comfortable and happy. It had indeed been followed by catastrophe and flood. The catastrophe of birth through which we all have most unwillingly to enter our new life. Then Miss Clarissa Nash who had

134 German: *world weariness.*
135 German: *the spirit who always denies.*

been drinking in every word of the first speaker, burst out almost in tears *"Oh what a dreadful come-down, etc. Surely it must be there, etc?"* I found the couple much more interesting and informative when their feet were on the ground.

[Next day] I called about 10.30am for my luggage and helped Georgia, who had had her breakfast, but not yet her bath, to prepare vegetables for dinner and the dried milk for Francesco's coffee and then found the two visitors and Mr Sloley in the Music Room. When the coffee came, there was a most interesting discussion about the prospects of obtaining domestic help in Britain after the war – apparently there is a proposal to bring over a number of black people to undertake all the menial jobs – this led on to the question of inter-marriage between black and white, to which both the Kennings, fresh from the States, were violently opposed – and introduced a still more practical solution, that of making our houses truly labour saving.

Monday 18 January, 1943

The German Bombers came to London again last night, by the light of the nearly full moon. As a reprisal for our terrific bombing of Berlin the night before. I woke with the siren, as it struck five on the cuckoo clock. It was strange to hear once more the wailing of the alarm taken up and echoed from village to village. I believe we hear it as far as Slough. Immediately after came the boom of our guns – not separate voices from which one could judge the place and the distance – but one continuous roar, like the sound of a terrific thunderstorm.

Saturday 30 January, 1943

Francesco told us a story of Schnabel [136], the famous pianist, whose playing by the way he entirely disapproves. Schnabel fancies himself on his playing of Chopin and gave a recital in which he pounded out the louder passages and thumped the others. He came into the green room very pleased with himself – saying *"my reading of Chopin is not sentimental but philosophical"*. *"Yes"*, said the pianist Rosenthal [137], who was present, *"Schopenhauer!"* [138]

136 Artur Schnabel (1882–1951).
137 Moriz Rosenthal (1862–1946).
138 Philosopher, Arthur Schopenhauer, was known for his pessimism.

Wednesday 10 February, 1943

I had my Italian lesson yesterday at the Studio when I came back last Friday Mother asked: *"and when am I going to see Francesco?"* I reminded her that Miss Barnes was going away soon for a week and that then Francesco would come here to give me my lesson, *"and will he stay the week?"* she asked. I told him this when I arrived yesterday and he was greatly moved and in a lovely spontaneous movement he kissed his hand towards Greylands and Mother. I asked him many things yesterday that I had wanted to know – about composition – whether he needed to wait till the inspiration came – or whether he chose a subject as a nucleus to group his music around. But the truth is in neither of these. He says his head is always full of music *"of no value"*, but every now and then a melody comes that he recognizes as worth preserving. So it happened one morning as he was getting out of bed. The air of his violin sonata sang itself in his mind and he said to himself *"that sounds like something worth keeping"*, and he wrote it down. *"And what happened to it?"*, I asked. He sent copies to Szigeti [139] and two other violinists but none of them would take any interest in it. Apropos of Laten he says he has lost very many pupils because he wouldn't prepare them for examinations. He says he believes in working without an exam in view, and if the pupil wishes to take it then let him. He says he knows he is preparing a terrible disappointment for his pupil Miss May – the very nice young girl who went with us to the Colensos, when I was staying at the Studio. She expects to become a prominent performer. He knows she will never be good enough and is feeling that he ought to tell her. I said she would find it out herself all in good time. Last Friday Muriel and Friend were at the Studio. Muriel is greatly changed and aged in appearance.

Sunday 21 February, 1943

They were coming to us to tea the following Wednesday but it rained too hard and they rang up to put it off after I had prepared a most wondrous tea. The following Wednesday Trina was down with 'flu. I met Muriel in grass green trousers and bright pink socks.

I haven't been writing this up, not because there was nothing to say, but because there was too much, so that I had not time to set it down. Miss Barnes departed on Wednesday to stay a week with old friends at Sydenham. She had put it off in order that Mrs Coleman could come to

139 Joseph Szigeti (1892–1973).

me, after Mr Coleman had had his ten days leave. But alas on the Friday, Mrs Coleman sent Mary in with a message that her husband was ill in bed with 'flu and she had sent for the doctor, in order to get his extension of leave, so would not be able to come to me. She has two landgirls lodging with her, in addition to the nice Irish Mary, who is employed cleaning buses at the Green Line Garage. They [land girls] are fetched in the morning and brought back at night in a lorry and have scarcely seen the country before. They are London girls with all the London attractions of lipstick make-up and nail dye. (Today our preacher was a Miss Smith, a big strapping girl with black hair and red cheeks, who works as a temporary postman!) Well, I didn't tell Miss Barnes, as I didn't want her to put off her holiday again, as I believe she would have done. But this had the important consequence that when the kitchen Ideal Stove went out, she left it full of ashes and anthracite for Mrs Coleman to clear out and the whole kitchen uncleaned and unpolished. So this was my first job the next morning. Every possible sort of job accumulated, most of them admitting of no delay. Two bags of bulbs arrived, the day after each other – too late I fear to be of much use. I ordered one bag last July. Lucy sent her alarm clock to me, to be mended by Mr Fountain with all possible haste, then called for by me, packed registered and despatched by post. But most exacting of all was a Ms [140] which I had promised to revise for Dr Grove, Francesco's great friend – he is a naturalised Austrian speaking the most perfect English – he gave the lecture on the last Sunday in January, and except for two tiny mistakes in pronunciation, there was nothing to suggest the fact that he is not an Englishman. Grove is a translation of his original name. He is lecturing to the troops, all up and down the country and never knows what sort of audience he will find. He was one of the lecturers on the Beveridge Plan [141], which so alarmed the War Office that they refused to let the soldiers either read or discuss it. I believe this taboo was taken off, however, after questions were asked in Parliament. Last week he was sent up to Scotland and found an audience of Polish Officers – most keen and intelligent. They had the lecture on China, that he gave us at the Studio. Well, a Czech author of the name of Sommers had written a book about the suffering of Czechoslovakia (Hungary and Bohemia) and asked Dr Grove to translate it, assuring him there was no hurry, then suddenly

140 Manuscript.
141 In 1942 Sir William Beveridge (1879–1963) proposed a scheme which was adopted post-war as National Insurance. Working citizens paid into a fund which then distributed benefits to the sick and unemployed.

he told him the publishers were demanding the book and would he please finish the translation in all haste. So then Dr Grove had to take the Ms about with him, making it in trains and without a dictionary – without time even to read over what he had written. Francesco gave him a map of the country between the Station and Greylands and marked Susan [142] on it so that I was amazed by Dr Grove greeting her by name when he arrived. We had a very happy evening, working at it together till 9.15pm with two meals interposed. About six Francesco rang up to know if I had killed his friend. He said he was really frightened! Dr Grove was to call for him at the Blacks where he had promised to attend a Labour Party Meeting, so we asked him to come here first to supper and let them go on together. *"But"*, said Dr Grove, *"he had promised to be there at half past seven and you know what he is..."* We worked on altering a noun here and a phrase there, till 9.15pm, when there was no more time to do anything but catch the train at 10pm. But we finished the allotted sixty pages. At 9.30pm Francesco rang up again from a kiosk in Green Lane, for the Blacks have no telephone. He said he was dying with sleep and fatigue. He had been up at 6am I knew and been in London till 6pm. However when I told him how well Dr Grove and I had got on he exclaimed. *"O you have made me so happy!"*. On a morning later he rang me up to say Dr Grove had written to him to give him the same report – saying *"Mabel ist ein reizender Mensch and ich habe der ganzen abend reichlich grossen"* [143] – when he rang off he said *"Goodbye reizender Mensch!"* [144]

Monday 1 March, 1943

I am writing this at Bertie's on the Monday morning – I couldn't come on Sunday, as Mother had been very poorly all week with lumbago. I had moved the sofa across the window on Tuesday so that she could have her hearing tube in the piano when Francesco played to her. It was a very cold raw day of east wind and I found her shivering with cold so the mischief was already done. However by Saturday she was nearly herself again and I started off by the 9.45am train, getting off at Finchley Road to leave Noel a pot of daffodils out of the garden. They had to be concealed in the deep shopping bag that Alice gave me at Christmas for we are no longer allowed to convey flowers or plants by rail, except in the form of a small posy. Last week two men were arrested at Paddington with I think £70 worth of

142 Mabel's dog.
143 Mabel is a lovely person and I had a great evening.
144 German: *charming man.*

daffodils in their suitcases, that they had brought up from Cornwall. They were heavily fined and the flowers confiscated and given to the hospital. Of course the idea is to keep the railways as free as possible for the conveyance of munitions. I found Noel very well and cheerful. He would have liked to meet us at Toynbee Hall,[145] but has an engagement at that hour. We had a little talk about Jews and I said I was rather ashamed but I do share the general instinctive prejudice. He says he feels it too, only that in the rare cases where a Jew is an idealist and not obsessed with the idea of getting on, he is the most beautiful character and staunch friend. He mentioned three men whom he said were amongst his best friends – Laski above all, Leonard Wolff[146] and another – these two were however a little spoiled by conceit. I got a bus all the way from Baker Street to Richmond Bridge. The spring is so early for we have had no winter except the one week of my holiday at the change of the year. In the blackest and slummiest corners of the Marylebone and Paddington Roads there were little almond trees in full bloom. I got to Bertie's in good time for lunch. She made me lie down in the afternoon and after tea we walked in the lovely gardens that slope down to the towpath and the river opposite these flats. They were full of spring, snowdrops nearly over, purple and yellow crocuses under the trees and in a rock garden some dwarf mauve azaleas in full bloom against the gray rocks. And now about Francesco's lecture recital. We got a train all the way from Richmond to Aldgate East, with only one change and got into Commercial Street about 1.40pm. As we walked along we came upon the Petticoat Lane Market shorn of most of its glory. *"To Toynbee Hall"* was marked up on a side street to the left. All the neighbourhood had been terribly bombed and there was a space in front of the Settlement Buildings where a bomb must have fallen, but the main building seems to be intact. It is a very modern and intricate assembly of rooms halls and staircases and was buzzing with all sorts of activities. There was to be a dramatic performance at three, the same hour as Francesco's lecture, with a ballet. The first person we met was a very tall and charming young man very scantily attired with bare legs, and when we went into the ladies room it was lined with charming young girls busily making up their faces before a round mirror. It was now 2.40pm, but the doors marked Music Room were still shut and my heart began to sink.

145 Toynbee Hall is a charitable institution in the East End of London.
146 Spelled Woolf (1880–1969) English political theorist, author, publisher (Hogarth Press) and husband of Virginia Woolf.

We went down the stairs again and met Francesco just turning into the courtyard, with Connie and someone whom I took to be her Mother.
At last they opened the doors but no audience appeared as yet. Bertie and I went in and took seats near the front and spent some time examining the grand piano. If I remember rightly, it was presented and decorated by William Morris. It is a Broadwood, in light wood, all adorned with panels painted mostly with standing female figures and continuous verses running round. Meantime people began to come in till in the end the good-sized hall was three parts full. Francesco says that Sarasate [147] used to travel round with a little group of friends to encourage him, and I was reminded of this as the hall filled up. Behind Bertie and me were Connie and her companion, behind them sat little Miss May, Francesco's fashionable London pupil, with her Mother and Father, who gave me a warm invitation to go to tea when I was in London. Then to my joy, Niso came in with his *"girl"* and we had a very nice chat. He is on night duty, from 8pm to 5am every night, at his hospital – not very good I think for such a boy. He is rather troubled about his hands, which are getting very hard and horny in the palms. His fiancée looks very nice, very young and shy. I was so glad to talk to her. And finally, the Eric Newton's came in and sat near the back (You remember she is Mrs Pearce's daughter). It is a most beautiful little hall, with a dais at one end where the piano stands. Here the walls are lined with linen-fold panelling. There was a very large blackboard waiting for Francesco. I think his lecture was a great success. He didn't seem at all nervous and looked very happy – used no notes and never hesitated for a word, and played most beautifully. The lecture was on Hayden and Mozart, and he played a sonata by each. Bertie was fascinated by Francesco. She says she has never met such a charming and lovable little man! She fell in love with Niso too, and was very happy and interested altogether. I don't think she gets many treats of this kind and did so appreciate it. It was a terrific day for Francesco. He played as usual at the Free Church in the morning, had no time for dinner but took sandwiches in the train, Toynbee Hall at three, no time for tea and Niso went with him in the train as far as Baker Street as the only chance for talk, Free Church again at 6.30pm, and weekly piano recital at the Blacks at 8pm.
And so to bed ....

147 Pablo de Sarasate (1844–1908). Spanish violinist and composer.

Friday 12 March, 1943

Thursday I devoted to cooking the dinner and tea at home for the Music Studio next day. Poor Georgia has been struggling against heart trouble and a threatened collapse ever since the Sunday of Francesco's lecture in London. He has been teaching all her pupils – cooking – Hoovering – and finally cleaning the windows of the music room. Friday he was to give his last Lecture Recital and Georgia was most anxious for it to be a success and to collect a good audience, but she was quite unfit to be up, let alone to play one piano with him in the Mendelssohn Concerto which was the main item in the musical programme. All this week a young Mrs Lockwood who lives just round the corner [148], has been seeing after their midday meal. She is an artist and although I did not know it, she is expecting her first baby in about two months. On the Thursday she was ill and in pain and could do nothing. I offered to manage the whole thing on Friday. They had asked little Miss May to come out that morning for her music lesson, stay to lunch and the lecture afterwards. Also the Warden of Toynbee Hall, Mr. Vanstone, had invited himself to the lecture and of course would stay to tea. I should have enjoyed the preparations the day before, if it had not been for Miss Barnes, who as usual was venomously opposed to my doing anything to help Mrs Pearce. I stood it as long as I could and then said I wished to hear not another word on the subject and would she kindly say no more. I was shaking as I said this and fully expected a re-doubled flow of eloquence, but to my amazement she did stop and with a sweet smile began (not to hold her peace – that is beyond her power) but to be eloquent on some other subject. I went off at 10.30am next morning – while Miss Barnes asked me as a parting shot if I had left anything for *"Mrs Brailsford and I"* for tea. *"I'll buy something while I am out,"* she said. As a fact I had left them half of all the cakes I had made and some very nice little tarts for dinner. I found Georgia just going to lie down in Francesco's room, bitterly cold with the fire unlit and as I came in she was saying to Mrs Lockwood, *"I don't know what we are to do about lunch. Will you see if you can buy a tart?"* So to my joy I was able to produce mine. After this, it was all fun and Miss Barnes receded into the background. Everything went as well as possible. There was a very good audience, and Mr Vanstone whom I sat next to, told me he would have made any effort not to miss the lecture. He was immensely interested in the two reasons which Francesco gave for the recent neglect of Mendelssohn, – one. The ill-favour in which everything early-Victorian

148 Pathside, Amersham.

had fallen, and two. the over-restraint that was characteristic of the Victorians. Mendelssohn he said could never let himself go, and consequently was never great. Mr Vanstone told me that his grandfather had been connected in some way with Windsor Castle and that he himself possesses several sheets of notepaper that Mendelssohn had decorated for Queen Victoria, with a stag head or similar creature copied from Landseer, and under it a few bars from one of his own works. Francesco told us that the Overture to the Midsummer Night's Dream was written when Mendelssohn was seventeen; and this the second greatest overture, in his opinion, in the literature of music. He made a most interesting comparison between him and Schubert, who he said was music and praeterea nihil [149] – with a life story of no interest and no other interest in his life. Eleven people stayed to tea. We had hot scones and ginger cakes and Mrs Lockwood poured out. After tea little Miss May helped me to wash up. Georgia used to be very shy of her. She thought she was just a *"high-flyer at fashion"*, but we know now that under her marvellously curled hair and her tigerskin coat and hat and her make-up, she is very simple very affectionate and very hard working. I was amazed when she told me yesterday that she had practiced daily between four to five hours: rises about 6.30am, gets the breakfast and does some housework, always getting to the piano at 9am. They have a daily help from ten to three. The Mother is a semi invalid and there is also a complete invalid, a distant relative living in the house for the duration. A nurse comes every day to look after her, except on Sundays, *"which day,"* said poor little Miss May, *"I dread because I have everything to do for her then, including putting her on the bed pan!"* As though all this were not enough, she turned up her very short skirt and showed me the daintiest silk petticoat that she had embroidered with dots and little flowers and this is the girl we thought was a society butterfly!

Monday 22 March, 1943

Yesterday was a concert at the Studio by the Italian violinist Angel Grande. He is a spare, handsome, rather colourless, middle-aged man – the very antipodes of Francesco. He has lived in England over twenty years, married to an English wife (not quite out of the top drawer, as Bertie would say!) but his English is so difficult to understand as to be impossible at a distance. Yet he is an indefatigable chatterbox! Georgia is fond of him for his generous admiration of Francesco and his bearing no grudge

149 Latin: and nothing more.

against him for the rather humiliating row they had on the occasion of their last concert. He insisted on editing some Classic they were to play together in what seemed to Francesco an immoral and indefensible way and the controversy waxed so hot between them that they parted and though Francesco afterwards gave way and played Mr Grande's version, he does not hold him in respect. On the other hand Grande has the greatest respect for him both as a pianist and a composer, and asked to be allowed to include his violin sonata in yesterday's programme. It was the only considerable item in it. The rest were very slight Spanish dances and a long arrangement from Corelli which Georgia accompanied. I enjoyed the Sonata very much, though it was so packed with themes that it was difficult to understand for the first time. It was also exceedingly difficult to play and Francesco broke off his practising of it one day saying he couldn't play it. *"Who wrote it?"* asked Georgia. The same drawback comes out in all his compositions. The trio for the three ladies really demanded three professional opera singers, and he has just had a letter from a conductor (Walter Ghörre?) [150] wishing to perform an orchestral piece of his, but regretting that all but the middle movement was too difficult. Francesco is going to see him tomorrow so I shan't have my Italian lesson till Thursday. He is going to propose to split up the score and give it to more instruments, so that they would not be overtaxed, and the conductor has also asked him to write something more for him. Angel Grande was very interesting at tea about the Spanish audiences. He says if a performer does not come up to expectation he must expect rotten eggs and tomatoes to be thrown at him, and though he may have pleased the audience four or five times, they will have no mercy if he fails on the 6th. They give no welcome when he steps on the platform. This is like what Francesco told us of the treatment to be expected by Italian lecturers. I wonder when we English began to deserve the reputation of a kindly people and how it came about? 200 years ago one hears and reads of a *"brutal populace"* – and they well deserved the adjective. This question is very insistent in my study for Charles Wesley.

Sunday 28 March, 1943

Sunday morning on Richmond Hill.

Yesterday was to me a revelation of the beauty of London. Bertie took me after tea for a long walk in Richmond Park. The sun was still shining but it was towards evening and all the country across the river was half hidden

150 Walter Goehr – known in England as George Walter.

in a grey and silver haze. The trees are almost bursting into leaf – in fact here and there we saw a lovely outline of branches and twigs tipped with bright green silhouetted against the misty distance. The chestnuts and here and there a magnolia in the full glory of the great white flowers. Richmond Park is not strictly a park at all – rather a great unspoilt common, dotted with very old thorn trees, some so old as to be gnarled and twisted as though by lightening, but hardly one that was not clothing itself in its spring green. We walked and sat and walked again, past patches of flowering gorse and happy dogs careered on the turf, digging for imaginary rabbits. I don't wonder they are excited, for the ground under our boot soles was springy like India rubber. Scotties were in the great majority. I had gone to Noel's flat on the way, but he had unfortunately gone out, but I left him the daffs and the bunch of lilies. I was glad to see he had no flowers, for a wonder – I hope not but rather fear that he would buy some on his way home, for this was the first day the ban had been taken off the flowers by rail and all the quite mean streets I passed through in the bus were gay with daffs and quite poor women carried bunches in their hands along with their shopping baskets: Noel's lady the Austrian, was very kind and brought me a bowl of hot soup, so I went on my way refreshed to Richmond.

Bertie and I got to Toynbee Hall [151] at about quarter to three, but there was nobody in the Music Room except the Warden who was very pleasant to us. Little by little the big hall became rather more than half full. Stella came in with a friend so I crossed over at once and gave her the bunch of daffs, to her great joy and they came back to sit beside Bertie and me. She designs dresses as well as being very much in the public eye as a lecturer and is always very fashionably dressed. I didn't care for her get up this time – it was a darkish red costume trimmed with little bands of green – what you call occurrences. Her hat was a flat sailor – all green except for strips of red. Her hair was in a wide meshed net and her hat tilted forward. She had very long silk legs! Bertie says her appearance was rather alarming and very Parisian! Her husband Eric Newton, came in later and had to sit by himself. *"Connie"* and little Miss May, sat just behind us and the fat pupil with spectacles. It was an audience mostly of very keen intelligent young people who asked most apposite questions when the time came. I heard that Francesco's Recital at Sutton the day before had been a very

151 Toynbee Hall is a charitable institution in the East End of London.

great success. He was very happy and played magnificently and what struck me perhaps most was his readiness in answering impromptu after the lecture any question put by the audience – such as would you consider Chopin a Nationalist composer?

The introduction was most interesting, explaining that no composer (I think the same may be said of a writer) can be judged out of his century and environment. He likened the great composers to tall trees – the lesser ones to shrubs – and quite minor ones to bacteria, who also, but only two thirds of them, played a useful part:

Bertie asked me to find a home for some theology documents relating to John Wesley, which have come to her thro' Will's stepmother, who was a Miss Suter, descended from one of Wesley's first preachers. There were five letters from Wesley himself – one written only a year before he died in a very shaky hand, seemed to be pure fun. Suter seems to have just got married and John Wesley says perhaps next midsummer day, after consulting with suitable *"sisters"* and if possible when the moon is full, he may be able to tell him the name of his wife! There are two letters from Dr. Coke, just starting on a missionary journey to India. The first is to Suter's son, urging him to give up his work and follow him (Dr Coke) as helper and fellow missioner. The second alas, is to Suter himself and begins *"Dear Brother, for so I must call you, in spite of your angry letter …"* Young Suter had been playing football, consequently even a fond father could not maintain, surely, that all his thoughts were Godward and that he was fit for the work of the Gospel. Since however, Mr Suter thought his son has been inspired (which he apparently was, as he had relinquished his employment to join Dr Coke). Dr Coke had ordered his bankers to pay them £14. This was written from Portsmouth on the eve of departure.

I want to try and give another little picture of Miss Barnes mentality. She was very keen last night to hear *"Everybody's Scrapbook"* on the wireless, so I turned it off in Mother's bedroom and left her to it. In the hall however, I could hear a very good snatch of violin and orchestra, which was cut off before one had fairly grasped what they were playing – to be succeeded by an account of Harvey and how he discovered the circulation of the blood. Miss Barne's came running to me and said *"O you must listen to this – it's all about ….*(Harvey I prompted her) *Yes, Harvey and how he discovered …* (MRB-the circulation of the blood) *Yes,"* said Miss Barnes *"and he dedicated it to Charles I and he was at the Battle of Edgehill and he hid his sons in a hedge, I should have thought everyone would have liked to listen, it teaches you such a lot!"* In a few minutes she very kindly came again and said, *"O do listen to this – it's about boomerangs and all that and a man tried to throw one and it didn't come back to him and it's all in the way you throw it, and there was a girl who sang a song about a boomerang and it's the only one that's ever been written! I can't understand you not listening!"*

I was treated at the Clinic by the handsome boy like Niso who is the son of Mr Leif of Champneys. [152] He is really called up to the Army, but has his call-up deferred till July so that he can take his final examination. He told me half in jest and half in earnest, that he is not however going to be called up. He has been to a Spiritualist séance, where the Medium asked the audience to give him some object of their person. He then being blindfolded, would read their character and destiny. Young Leif's pencil was the first and the Medium exclaimed, *"It's very strange, but I see the person to whom this pencil belongs surrounded by sick and suffering people. A great change will come in his life next June."* *"Yes,"* said young Leif, *"I am expecting to be called up."* *"I can't see any trace of uniform in your future,"* said the Medium.

Saturday 3 April, 1943

I think my life is rather like the book of Dr Sommer that I have been revising for Victor Grove. It is lived in isolated chapters, differing totally in atmosphere and context with only the one slender connection that all the events happen to the same person. Yesterday (Saturday) I was invited to supper at 6.30pm at the Studio to meet Victor. He and his wife and Francesco all arrived together. The wife is a very nice-looking Jewess, very short with beautiful dark blue eyes and black frizzy hair. She comes from Switzerland or Austria, and has a poor command of English. But she too is a very successful lecturer – exclusively to Jews, on the subject of 'Zionism'. Victor has just come back from lecturing to the troops at Dover. He says two thirds of the original inhabitants have been evacuated but the town is full with the navy and the army. There are constant alerts and air raid warnings. He was told that when a dull lecturer was sent and the men were observed to be slipping out of the hall, the authorities would give orders for the barracks siren to be sounded. Thereupon of course the audience was obliged to rush out to man the anti-aircraft guns, and the lecture came to an end, without the speaker feeling wounded! Francesco had another

152 Champneys is situated between Chesham and Tring. It was known then as a Nature Cure Resort.

equally funny story, on a different plane. Last week he was to have gone on Tuesday to interview Dr. Walter Goehr, but the meeting was put off till the Thursday week (last Thursday) because he was ill. It appears he had gone to Champneys three weeks ago, suffering from neuralgia in the face. The charge was twelve guineas a week and he was put through the usual course of one starvation, two fruit juice, three milk. At the end of the week he felt better in himself but the neuralgia had not abated and Mr Leif said he must go on as before. Finally someone suggested he should see a dentist. A bad tooth was extracted and next day he was perfectly well. He approved of Francesco's proposal to make his music easier by splitting it up amongst more instruments and promised to bring it out in public. He is, it seems, well known as a conductor. He figures in BBC programmes as John [sic] Walter and has been conducting at the Albert Hall.

Francesco is beginning to believe, though with much trembling that his luck has returned. Mr Vanstone asked him last Sunday to give a course of lecturers at Toynbee Hall and four days later he gets a promise of his concerto being performed. He is most eager to get it finished. He was very tired last night after getting up at 6am and having a day of teaching and playing in Town, but he said he could not sleep unless he had done some work at it, and sat up till ten 'oclock writing the new score. He and Victor played two sonatas for Violin and Piano – Mozart and Beethoven. At 9.15pm I said I must go but they urged me to stay the night and Francesco rang up Miss Barnes to say they had persuaded me to do so as the night was so dark - and so it was, like a thick black curtain against the window. As the Groves were going to their sleeping place, with some friendly neighbours, he presented me with a lovely little copy of the Divine Commedia, bound in ivory vellum, and with a very quaint brass box made of tiny carved peacocks – an Indian piece of work for holding spices I think. I slept on the stretcher at the other end of the music room and my one regret was the absence of my toothbrush! I walked home across the fields after breakfast in the early sunshine and found Miss Barnes to my great surprise very amiable and glad I had not come home in the dark!

Monday 19 April, 1943

Miss Barnes has just said she heard Dr Ticciati playing.
"He has a nice touch hasn't he? He plays well."

Wednesday 28 April, 1943

I had a great excitement this morning as I lay in bed. I heard a very loud cuckoo and looked through the uncurtained window, to see him on one of the lower boughs of the acacia tree. A great bird about the size of a pigeon. He was silhouetted against the early morning sky, so I can't be quite sure, but he appeared to have a grey chest and black wings which he carried drooping at his sides. Before he flew off he cuckooed five times (it should have been seven!) and then I saw how exact a copy is his effigy in the cuckoo clock. Each time he shouted he bowed his body and flapped his wings and I could clearly see his big beak wide open to let out the great sound.

We have had Lucy for Easter. She wanted nothing but to stay in bed and rest, which she did from Thursday to Tuesday. We were grieved to see her so very tired. She has had no help of any kind in her housework for over a year, and does it I think far too slowly and for too conscientiously.

Monday 3 May, 1943

Connie and Francesco are coming this evening for their first talk on English Literature.

Thursday 6 May, 1943

I saw Mrs Coleman this morning. Mr Coleman's commanding officer has persuaded him to apply for a commission and thinks he is sure to get it. He himself fears that his lack of education will stand in his way, but she says he is in very high favour just now. He and a number of other Commandos were up in a balloon, and were ordered to make their descent in full kit with their heavy boots. The men all refused, but Mr Coleman asked them to follow him and he jumped and the other men followed. He sent Mrs Coleman a paper which had to be signed by some one of the dignitaries specified, to the effect that they had known him for a least four years, and could testify to his good moral character. He is coming home on leave next week and will take Mrs Coleman to Yeovil, while Mary goes to her grandmother at Penn. Today has been very strange. While Miss Barnes was away I cleared the kitchen and sitting room grates in preparation for the sweep who was to come at eight this morning. Mother got settled in my bedroom before breakfast and I prepared the two rooms and helped Miss Barnes with the kitchen. When the sweep, who was due at eight, had not appeared by 9.30pm I rang up his house at Chesham. His wife looked up his engagement book and found that he was booked to come to us on Wednesday a week hence, and not today! So of course I had to put off Mrs Coleman who was to begin our spring cleaning tomorrow. It must now be postponed for three weeks, when Mr Coleman will have come and gone. We had dinner early, so that I might have a rest before going to the dentist, where I believed I had an appointment at 2.30pm. But when I got up there the secretary looked up the engagement book, and found that I was booked for Friday at 2.30pm and not today. Surely this doesn't often happen twice in a couple of hours? Yet a third engagement was altered last night, but all to the good! Francesco rang up to know if they might come on Saturday afternoon for the English lesson instead of Monday evening as this would give more time and he could *"combine a concert for Mother!"*

Monday 10 May, 1943

I wanted to consult with Noel about your birthday and we decided to ask you if what we had in mind would be what you would like? I thought it would be nice to ask Mr Reed to come for the weekend (Noel would pay his fare and he would sleep two nights in my room) and Noel says we should invite Dr Bond and Ernest French to come for part of Saturday. Of course they could get home the same night. Would you like this? If so, I will write to them all at once, so that they can clear the way. [153]

I was at Mr Wege the dentists on Friday, and found that he was going back on Tuesday into the Navy. He served in it through the last war, volunteering from South Africa at the age of sixteen. He volunteered again as soon as this War broke out, but was rejected on account of his age and the useful work he was doing. Now however, the age limit has been widened and he has been accepted, with the title of Surgeon Lieutenant. He is leaving a wife and three children at home. Many years ago, at his request, I vetted his autobiography as far as it went: now he says he is going again to keep a diary and will ask me to make a book of it – á la Mrs Van der Elst!

Wednesday 26 May, 1943

We had a delightful little flying visit from Dr Bond [154] on Sunday afternoon. He was preaching at High Wycombe and came the ten or twelve miles bus ride, with his host, staying ten minutes with Mother and taking

153 Written for her Mother to read and make decisions about her 100th birthday celebration.
154 Rev. Dr. Robert Bond (1894-1952), President of Methodist Conference 1938.

the bus back. He had scarcely gone – not even giving me the chance of producing the very nice tea I had prepared for him the day before – when Mr & Mrs Lilienfeld came in and stayed an hour. He is very friendly and even affectionate but I fear I don't love him. It is strange to me that such an intensely musical man should be so prosaic! Francesco and Connie and I are having very happy times over our English Literature. It is marvellous to me that they are both so keen to come. Connie had been spending the weekend with Francesco's old pupil, Miss Rose, at her cottage in the Isle of Wight It is of course a prohibited area and they had to go through a strict interrogation by a policeman when they got off the boat. Miss Rose had to prove that she was going to visit her own property and Connie was asked if she was a near relative. However they let her through. Francesco has invited us both to Priestley's new play *"They Came to a City"* at the Globe theatre. [155]

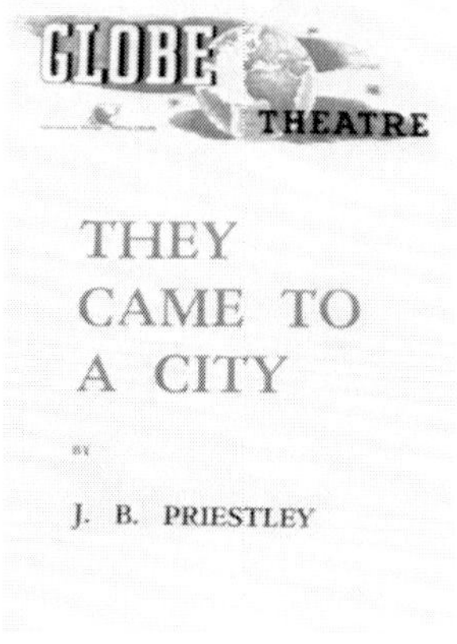

He will meet me at Baker Street (he goes at 7.30am for economy, he says that when he does this he feels he earns the right to spend money on treats) and we will go by invitation to Miss Rose's house on Camden Hill for tea. She and I met in the Studio kitchen after Gabrielle May's [156] recital and it seems she liked me. Connie will meet us at the theatre and go back to sleep at Miss Rose's. Georgia had lent me a Life of a French Curé who was recently canonized (The making of a Saint, by John Oxenham) [157] and we were talking about the use of hair shirts and flagellation to subdue the flesh. I said I had no idea that they were practiced in modern days. Francesco told us then that when he and his sister had been naughty, they used to hear their Mother scourging herself in her room after they had gone to bed.

155 The programme (illustrated) had been inserted in the journal.

156 It is not clear whether Gabrielle May is a relative of Richenda May or whether she got the first name wrong and they are one and the same.

157 Oxenham, John.(1852-1941) *A Saint in the Making.*

Tuesday 25 May, 1943

After making our two beds and doing our usual jobs in the bedroom I cooked the dinner (bread pudding, cabbage and cheese semolina) then I weeded in the back garden and planted some seeds. Rested after lunch and then did a considerable ironing of under clothing towels and pinafores that I washed yesterday. After that I cut sandwiches for tea. After tea I had nearly two hours at Charles Wesley. I am now typing the first four chapters. I helped Miss Barnes get the supper and after it I syringed the roses and did a little more weeding.

Thursday 27 May, 1943

Francesco has just rung up to say that Dr Victor Grove is coming to spend Sunday with him and may he bring him to tea – so I asked Mrs Pearce as well. Francesco said they wanted me to go to them, but knew I couldn't because of Miss Barnes, but he says he and Victor will get the tea and they will wash up. I unfortunately told Miss Barnes what he said and she is so angry. She doesn't want anyone messing about in her kitchen!

postscript

The journal ends abruptly at the bottom of the last page of the third notebook. The narrative probably continued in another notebook which has not survived. It would have been interesting to read an account of Clara's hundredth birthday party a month later, although there is a brief description of the occasion from Mabel's cousin Bertie, who wrote a 'thank you' note to Mabel, Bertie said: *"I do hope the beloved little Aunt was no worse for the excitement and influx of visitors on Sunday. It was a joy to see her looking so well and happy – and such an event in the lives of all who love her. I hope too that you were not quite tired out. I was all so delightful and the lovely tea – and such a fine warm day. Everything conspired to make it all such a delightful day."*

The local newspaper printed a picture of Clara for her hundredth birthday and a summary of her life which included her famous Son, and her industrialist Father, but sadly no mention of her devoted daughter.

Mabel was cut out of the published photo.

Mabel Brailsford's journal gives us a glimpse of Mabel's personality and intellect. Being an accomplished pianist herself she admired the musicians and singers that frequented the Music Studio. She enjoyed the intellectual stimulation of the Sunday talks as well as the various musical events she attended. She was obviously proud of her Brother's achievements and she glowed when he complimented her. However the narrative suggests that Mabel was more of an observer of life, than a participant. Her solicitude towards her Mother, and her willingness to help neighbours and friends demonstrated her desire to gain self-worth through the approval of others.

In the journal we met the bombed out evacuees, Mr and Mrs Lewis, who were billeted with Mabel and Clara. Looking after the expanded household proved too exhausting for Mabel, and the Lewises moved to a new billet on 24 August 1941. However they continued to visit Mabel and Clara, and in the journal there is a letter from Mrs Lewis, postmarked 24 March 1943, from an address in North London.

"My Dear Mabel,

Just a line trusting that both you, and your Dear Mother are quite well, I am pleased to say that I am completely settled having got a permit for the utility furniture, which is quite good, which was really a blessing so now my home will be complete within the next few weeks, they allowed me a dining table four chairs, two nice large armchairs (silk tapestry), and a divan for Arthur to sleep on when on leave. I managed to buy a sideboard and a bedroom suite (very good ones) through Mr Lewis's nephew who are [sic] in the trade. So you see I haven't done too bad, thank the Almighty. I am pleased to say Arthur is quite well and managed to get four days leave, to come and see us. You can just imagine how relieved he was to know that at last we have really a home of our own, and such a nice flat, which you must see, some day. We shall always be pleased to see you, by the way, did you have a holiday and sincerely hope you are all the better for it. I might add Arthur has been shifted to Wilts where he is training for Flying Control, Air Navigation and weather forecasting for six months, after a certain amount of flying, they have six months on the ground staff. What he is doing is very important job.
He has to be very accurate. He really leads the Airman all the way when on flights, he is in contact with them all the time, on the wireless in case of emergency, should they get lost he has to guide them back and tell them the way. So you can see what a very responsible job it is. I am certain he can do it as he has always done extremely well in whatever he has undertaken, and we are really very proud of him, doing his best for his Country (God Bless Him) and he looks exceedingly well and is certainly working his way up. He always sends his love to both your Mother and yourself, and will never forget how kind you were to Mr Lewis and myself. Well Cheerio Dear, hoping all is well with kindest regards to your Dear Mother and yourself in which Mr Lewis and Arthur joins.

I remain yours very sincerely.

(Mrs) C Lewis

P.S.
Please give my kind regards to Miss Barnes and hope she is well."

Mabel's indignant reaction to being addressed familiarly as *"Mabel"* by Mrs Lewis, especially as she referred more formally to Miss Barnes, can only be imagined.

Mabel's relationship with Miss Barnes appears to grow into mutual dependency over the years. Although irritated by Miss Barnes' opinions and lack of intellectual knowledge, Mabel would not have had the freedom to write and visit her friends without Miss Barnes willingness to *"baby sit"* her Mother. Sometimes, in the journal, Mabel almost treats her as live-in help. At one point Mabel says *"I let Miss Barnes out for the day"*, but at other times she seems to derive some amusement from her utterances. A lack of personal information about Miss Barnes, especially her first name has prevented any further research into this lady.

Mabel's grief at her Mother's death in November 1944 at the age of 101 must have been overwhelming. After a lifetime as her Mother's companion she was now alone. Her friends and neighbours would have been supportive, but more misery was to come. Mabel's friend, Emily Bolam, for whom she had *"an admiration for her that has gone on growing"* died barely a month later on 27 December 1944. The friendships of people she met at the Music Studio, together with her great admiration of Francesco Ticciati, would have been a great comfort, but Francesco's death in 1949 aged 55, must have been devastating. She remained close to her Brother. He had married a young German refugee just before their Mother's death. During his frequent bouts of ill-health the young wife took over his nursing care, but in 1952 when his heart was so weak he was unable to manage stairs or walk far he moved into Mabel's bungalow.

Once again, for nearly six years Mabel had the role of devoted companion. Although unable to leave the house H.N. Brailsford continued to write for the New Statesman, recorded talks for the BBC, and worked on his book. His wife would visit at weekends, but during the week Mabel and her Brother listened to music, read together, and had a succession of scholarly visitors still eager to discuss world affairs with him. He was writing a large historical work called The Levellers and the English Revolution, which had been in progress for many years and which was published after his death.

When Mabel's Brother died in hospital in March 1958 at the age of 84 Mabel was 82 and totally alone for the first time in her life. Mabel lived for another twelve years. Many of the people mentioned in the journal left Amersham after the war and she outlived many others. Her Will contains bequests to those that were close to her in her later years. She had a live-in companion/carer, Dorothea Becker, and the friendship of her sister-in-law and Mr and Mrs Burrows. It is hoped that her indomitable spirit remained with her until the end. After her death Greylands was demolished and two detached houses were built on the same plot.

Mabel spent her life in the shadow of her much applauded brother. Apart from her published books Mabel Brailsford's existence might have gone unrecognised if it were not for the discovery of her journal, which has shown her to be intelligent, witty and insightful. This lucid and entertaining account of her thoughts and descriptions of events and people have given us a vivid account of life in a small town during World War Two.

appendix

Appendix of Biographies of People mentioned in the Diary

These biographies have been compiled and researched from available sources. They are based mainly on Mabel's spellings and her perceived knowledge of the individual. All effort has been made to keep them accurate and where doubts about accuracy occur they are mentioned. Only non-living personnel have been recorded.

Adelaide

A relative of Mabels who lives in Oldham.

Alexander, Miss

Flamboyant visitor to the Music Studio. [unable to trace]

Barnes, Miss

Bombed out evacuee from London. Billeted at Greylands 1941–1943 and possibly longer. Her first name is unknown. She visited friends in Sydenham, and had a two-week holiday with her brother in London. [unable to trace]

Barrett, Mr and Mrs John

Malvern, London Road East. Mabel's neighbours.

Beakbane, Nance 1877–1943

Real name Hannah Beakbane, a Quaker living in the Quaker village of Jordans. Mabel knew many people from the Society of Friends, and it is possible that she knew "Nance" from her researches which lead to the writing The Making of William Penn and Quaker Women. Hannah was born in Lancashire in 1877, went to a Quaker boarding school in Somerset with her two sisters, and travelled widely. She never married and died in Amersham at the beginning of 1943 aged 66.

Bertha

Visitor to the Music Studio. A member of the congregation of the Order of the Cross

Bertie

Cousin of Mabel's. Lived at 7 Glenmore House, Richmond Hill, Surrey. Bertie attended Clara's 100th Birthday party. Bertie told Mabel she was pleased to meet *"unknown and very rich relations at the 100th birthday party especially the three men"*.

Black, Mr and Mrs Charles

Lived at 53 Woodside Road, Amersham. Mr Charles Black, a mathematician, was a Grammar School Maths teacher, and working for Mrs Churchill's Aid to Russia Fund. His wife, Phyllis, a teacher, were Labour Party supporters and music lovers. They had two boys, John and Leo, who were 11 and 10 at the time of the diary. Mr Black was a Senior Wrangler, a term given to the top-scoring student with First Class Honours in the Mathematics Tripos degree at Cambridge for his year. They had a grand piano upon which Francesco Ticciati practised when he first came to Amersham and was first billeted at Flint House in Woodside Road. It was Mrs Black who introduced him to Mrs Pearce and he later moved into the Music Studio. Mr Black was a friend of H.N. Brailsford from when they had served together on a Labour Spain Committee which Brailsford chaired.

Blairgowrie

Mabel Brailsford's parents were living at Rosebank Manse, Balmoral Road, Blairgowrie in 1891. Her father was the Wesleyan Methodist Minister. The House is now a hotel and a listed building. Mabel was at a Methodist Boarding School at Southport, Lancashire at that time and visited her parents in the school holidays.

Blatchford, Robert 1851–1943

Socialist campaigner, journalist, and author. Set up the socialist newspaper, The Clarion, a rival to the Labour Leader edited by H.N. Brailsford.

Bolam, Emily 1891–1944

George and Emily Bolam were Wardens at Friends House, Whielden Street. George Bolam, a carpenter and joiner, helped build Jordans Village for the Jordans Village Trust. He and Emily, a fellow Quaker, married in 1921 and moved into the unoccupied Amersham Meeting House and set about renovating the Meeting House. George Bolam had a woodworking workshop in Church Street and after his death his sons donated his woodworking tools to the Amersham Museum. George and Emily had three sons, John, David, and Godfrey.[1] Godfrey Bolam describes his Mother as having *"a certain cachet in the district because she was 'educated' (a B.A. degree from Bedford College, London) and women graduates were a rarity in those days."* Emily opened a branch of the County Library in a room adjoining the Friends Meeting House. [see Library]

Bond, Rev. Dr Robert

Leading Wesleyan Minister and President of the Methodist Conference 1938.[2]

Bondfield, Miss

Office manager of a [London] Metropolitan Council. The Council office was evacuated to Copperkins Lane, Amersham. Miss Holmes worked for her.

Bone, Sir Muirhead 1876–1953

War Artist. Family friend of the Brailsfords. Sir Muirhead Bone died in 1953 in Oxford. He has a memorial stone in St. Paul's Cathedral in London.

Bone, Gertrude 1876–1962

Wife of Muirhead Bone, poetess and author. Daughter of a Wesleyan minister and sister of Francis Dodd, the portrait painter.

Bone, Gavin David 1907–1942

Gavin David Bone son of Gertrude (Author) and Muirhead Bone (war artist). They had another son, Stephen who was also an artist. In 1939 Gavin had an M.A. and was Fellow and Lecturer in English at St John's College, Oxford University.

Boughton, Joy

Played Flute. Part of a Trio at the National Gallery. Her Father was Rutland Boughton, 1878–1960.

Bowen-Davies, Eileen 1902–1975

Lived with her parents at The Old Garden, South Park, Gerrards Cross.

1 Bunney, George. Life and work of Amersham Meeting from 1917 until 1939. Amersham Friends House 2008

2 The Daily Mail, 16/1/1937, p.3.

Brailsford, Edward James

Mabel's Father.
Wesleyan Methodist
Minister, Author.

Brailsford, Noel

Mabel's brother. H.N. Brailsford, Journalist, author, broadcaster. Henry Noel Brailsford was born on Christmas Day 1873. He travelled widely, observing and writing about politics, oppression, and injustice. Whilst at Glasgow University his intellectual talents began to emerge and he seemed destined for an academic career as a classicist and philosopher. However, in 1897 he volunteered to fight for Greece in their war with Turkey. Whilst there he sent back first hand accounts of the war to the Glasgow Daily Herald and returned from the conflict wounded and with *"distaste for excessive patriotism and the brutality of war"*. From this developed his dislike of oppression and he became an active campaigner on various issues. He was a member of the Conciliation Committee for Women's Suffrage, and as a journalist he campaigned tirelessly on behalf of social issues that he felt strongly about. In many ways his thinking was ahead of his time and was thought too radical to be taken seriously. During the First World War he pushed for a negotiated settlement, and wrote A League of Nations in 1917, proposing a democratic federation of Nations who could settle their differences diplomatically. It was well received, and American President, Woodrow Wilson, sent a confidant to London to interview Brailsford and other like-minded people. In 1918 Brailsford was a member of the Family Endowment Committee which proposed the establishment of a national scheme of payments made directly to Mothers for each of her children. It was not until 28 years later that Family Allowances were introduced. In 1919 he was one of the first journalists to tour war-torn Europe. He lobbied for an easement in the terms of the Treaty of Versailles, fearing the poverty and wretchedness of the situation in Germany would get out of control. In 1922 he was appointed Editor of the weekly New Leader published by the Independent Labour Party. He was an executive member of the India League which was committed to total independence. At this time he was unofficial assistant editor at the New Statesman, and at the same time he was broadcasting talks on BBC radio. By 1940 his American articles in the New Republic were urging for American entry into the war. In May 1941 the Ministry of Information authorised his passage to New York and Washington as a New Statesman correspondent, and also to lobby informally for American Intervention. At the end of January 1958 Brailsford suffered a coronary thrombosis and was admitted to Hammersmith Hospital where he died.

Brailsford, Clara 1843–1844
Mabel and Noel's Mother. Born 27 June 1843 the 9th child of Henry Pooley of Liverpool, an ironfounder and engineer who made his fortune with the birth of the railways and their need for accurate weighing machines. Mabel was Clara's companion for the whole of her life.

After Mabel's father died in Ilfracombe they moved to Little Elms, London Road East, Amersham, and sometime in the early 1930s moved to Greylands. In a letter Noel writes to his Mother around 1935 he says he is looking forward to *"inspecting the changes at Greylands and presenting the cottage to them with his love"*, which suggests he helped them financially.

Bunney, Mrs Helen
Helen Bunney and her husband John Bunney lived in Mitchell Walk, Amersham. They were members of the Society of Friends. John was a Chartered Accountant and a Member of the Parish Council. They had four children: John, George, Elizabeth and Helen.[3] In a recent interview with George Bunney he stated that the views expressed by Mabel Brailsford about his father, whilst not true, were just her personal opinions.

Burrows, Mrs
Singer. Married to Keith Burrow. Alias Pixie, alias Carol Squires. Mabel describes meeting them at the Music Studio. They lived in West Middlesex. The friendship with Mabel must have continued after the War as Mabel left them a bequest in her will.
Mrs Burrows, stage name Carol Squires was a member of the BBC singers at that time.

Burrows, Mr Keith
Blind concert pianist. As well as performing at the Music Studio and giving live concerts with his wife around the country, he also broadcast performances on the BBC Home service. He was also a music teacher.

Bush, Miss
Evacuee staying at the Dawsons house. She was a school-teacher at The Chiswick High School for Girls which had been evacuated to Amersham and used Challoner's facilities in the afternoons. The school returned to London in September 1942.

Busoni, Ferruccio 1866–1924
Italian composer, pianist, conductor, editor, writer and piano teacher.

Canetti, Elias
Bulgarian refugee billeted with Gordon Milburn at this time. He wrote about his life in Amersham in Party in the Blitz. He was awarded Nobel prize for Literature in 1981.

Cavalho, Mrs
"handsome loud looking Portuguese Jewess". This might be Rachel Cavalho who lived in Maida Vale where Ticciati used to live.

3 Bunney, George. Life and work of Amersham Meeting from 1917 until 1939 Amersham Friends House 2008.

Champion, Miss
Miss Champion, lived at Westover, Station Road, Amersham. Her house was considered as a potential billet for the Lewises.

Charleville Mansions
Barons Court, London.
Thought to be where cousin Lucy Knowles used to live.

Clegg, Mr
Possibly a Methodist Minister.
He told Mabel about his son in Libya.

Cipriax, Dr
Chiropractor in London

Clibborn Arnold 1883–1964
Wife Jocelyn 1897–1968.
They lived at Gwern-y-Glyn, Dolywern, Wrexham, North Wales.
There is a letter from them in Mabel's papers. Mabel appears to have known them before the war when they lived in Birkenhead.

Coke, Dr Thomas 1747–1814
First Wesleyan Bishop.
His world-wide missionary voyages led to him being known as the Father of Methodist Missions.

Coleman, Mr and Mrs and Mary
Edward William Coleman, Penwarne, London Road East. Neighbours.

Colenso, Irma 1855–1959
Irma married Angelo Crovo at the end of 1933, having been born in Norwich in 1885. Her Grandfather was John William Colenso, the Bishop of Natal. Her Father, Francis Ernest Colenso, was a barrister in Natal, but returned to work in England. He continued to campaign for the rights of the Zulu people. Her Mother was Sophia Jeanette Frankland Colenso. Both her parents died in Amersham. Their house was Elangani in Chestnut Lane.
Mr Bunney remembers that they sometimes had musical evenings at their house.

Corelli, Arcangelo 1653–1713
Italian violinist and composer.

Crawshaw, Mrs Ellen Elizabeth
1848–1942
Mabel attended her Quaker funeral.
She lived at Green View, Jordans, Buckinghamshire.

Crovo, Angelo 1867–1957
Husband of Irma Colenso. The Crovo's were known to Elias Canetti. He recalls, *"It was Mr Crovo I spoke to on my very first visit to Amersham. I did not know my way around at all. On Chestnut Lane, I met a man with a round blond head and bright eyes, not at all old. I asked him the way to Stubbs Wood. He offered to show me a shortcut through his overgrown garden, through all sorts of shrubs and bushes. He was very chatty … and told me he was Romanian and was an oil engineer who had come to England in his early years…"*

Daisy Shop
43 High Street.
Trade directory shows Mrs Compton as the owner, china dealer.

Danziger, Freda 1888–1970
[Actual spelling Frida Dancyger]
Billeted at Flint House, Woodside Road, Amersham. It was a guest house at that time. An accomplished singer. She was born in London. Her Father was a Jewish Minister from the Russian-ruled partition of Poland. He probably emigrated to London to escape the Russian Pogroms at the end of the 19th Century. According to Electoral registers she shared her North London living accommodation with Violet Defries. One of her many singing engagements was at the West London Synagogue where Ticciati played.

Dawson, Albert Mason Patrick
1881–1963
Willowdene, London Road East.
Civil servant. Published writer of poetry and morality plays.

Defries, Violet 1871–1948
Mezzo-soprano, drawing room reciter, singing teacher, writer, bird imitator, poet. Friend and flatmate of Frida Dancyger. Her portrait was painted by Frank Markham and published in the Strand magazine of December 1893 alongside other *"beauties"*. Another portrait of her, this time by Mr Skipworth was exhibited at the Grosvenor Gallery in 1889 and described as *"she is not weakly pretty, but rightly handsome"*. She wrote for the Pall Mall Gazette, and directed an amateur Dramatic Society of the Jewish Working Men's Club in 1898. She produced a London musical in 1895.

Downer, Mrs
[unable to trace]

Druces's shop
Baker Street, London.

Dupré, Connie [Dupree] 1913–1967
Francesco's French pupil.
Lived with her parents, Frank and Florence at Aberdovey, Pineapple Road, Amersham.

Durdac, M.
Noel's French teacher at Dundee High School.

Ellis, Mr and Mrs John George and son Lawrence.
Lived at Elmcroft London Road East. Neighbours. They used to live in the High Street, Amersham. Mr Ellis worked for the GPO and died in 1941 after an accident.

Elst, Mrs Violet Van Der 1882–1966
Millionairess. Eccentric. Anti-Capital Punishment. See The Incredible Mrs Van Der Elst, Charles Neilson Gattey. Leslie Frewin of London, 1972.

Epstein, Jacob 1880–1959
British Sculptor. Knighted in 1954. His work is displayed all over the world.

Esplin, Mabel
Both Mabels were at Wintersdorf School, Trafalgar Road, Birkdale Lancs in 1891. Mabel Esplin was born Manchester in 1875.

Essex, Mrs
Albert William Essex and his wife and three-year-old son, Norman, lived at Stonygreen, London Road East. Mabel's neighbours.

Evans, Mary
Dance teacher. Member of Mrs Pearce's church, the Order of the Cross.

Exell, Mrs
Lived at Little Elms, London Road East. The house where Mabel and Clara lived when they first came to Amersham.

French, Ernest
Not found, but possibly linked with Dr Bond and the Wesleyan Methodists.

Friends Meeting House
Whielden Street, Amersham.
The Bolam family lived there as Wardens. From time to time it was the venue for speakers of the Pacifist persuasion. Godfrey Bolam remembers John Middleton Murry was one and possibly Vera Brittain.

Friends Meeting House
Jordans, Buckinghamshire.
Mabel attended Mrs Crawshaw's funeral there. One of the oldest Friends meeting House in the country and still in use. William Penn and other early Quakers are buried there.

Forward, Stanley
Accountant. Recording Clerk.
Member of the Society of Friends.
At Quaker funeral.

Fountain, Mr
Clock repairer.
There are several Fountains in Amersham at that time. This might be Herbert Fountain (1880 –1951) who did cycle repairs at 92 High Street, Amersham. He also sharpened lawn mowers and was a jobbing gardener.

Franck, César 1822–1890
Composer, pianist, organist.

Glover, Mr Arthur Herbert
Herbert and Marjorie Glover, Martindale, London Road East.
Mr Glover died of pneumonia in 1941. They had two boys that went to Berkhamsted School, one of which had asthma. They had a goat called Jill. According to Mabel Marjorie did not get on well with her Mother.

Glover, "Old" Mrs
Must be the mother-in-law of Marjorie.

Goehr, Walter 1903–1960
German-born Composer and Conductor who came to London in 1937. As well as conducting major orchestras for live and recorded music he also wrote the film score for Great Expectations (1946) starring John Mills. He conducted the orchestra for original film scores written by his friend, Allan Gray, an Amersham resident, such as A Matter of Life and Death (1946). Leo, the son of Mr and Mrs Charles Black, recalls him living in Amersham during the war. He does not appear in any local directories so must have been an evacuee. Also known in England as George Walter.

Gordon West, Mrs
[unable to trace]

Gort, Viscount
Army General.
[6th Viscount Gort, 1886–1946]

Goulter, Mr Albert Manning
Chief Warden.
Lived at Aldercar, Stanley Hill.

Grande, Angel 1895–1951
Spanish violinist.

Green, Dr Edwin
In partnership with Dr Henderson at the surgery at Market Square Amersham. Lived at Netherlands, Station Road.

Green, Margaret
Possibly Margery Glover's mother.

Green, Min
[unable to trace]

Grove, Dr Victor 1889–1944
Writer and Lecturer. Friend of Ticciati. Buried in the churchyard of All Saints Parish Church, Wokingham, Berks.

Henderson, Dr Henry John M.C., M.B., B.S.Lond., M.R.C.S. Eng., L.R.C.P.Lond.
(Practice name: Henderson and Green). Physician, surgeon, medical officer and public vaccinator No. 44 district, Amersham Area Guardians Committee. Lived at Alwyns, Cokes Lane, Chalfont St Giles; and had surgeries at, Market Square, Amersham and Bank Chambers, High Street, Great Missenden.
Mabel practically accuses him of malpractice, but was probably unaware that he was a war hero. As Lieutenant Henderson, MB, RAMC he received the Military Cross in 1918. The descript on of his gallant action said,
"He established his aid post within 300 yards of the enemy's position and dressed and evacuated cases in the open. It was due to his splendid example, cheerfulness, and courage that a great number of lives were saved."
[4] After being gassed he returned to England and worked at the Central Military Hospital, Eastbourne before returning to his practice in Amersham. As a result of the gassing Dr Henderson could have been suffering from a chronic condition which could explain his apparent truculence.

Hill, Mr
Connected with Methodist Chapel, High Street, Amersham.
Possibly her neighbour at Larklands, London Road East.

Hoby, James
Wesleyan Minister. Grandfather of Mrs Pearce and trustee of the Wesleyan Methodist Chapel at Great Queen Street Chapel, London. Related to Sir Thomas Hoby 1530 –1566 of Bisham Abbey.

Holmes, Miss
Staying at Willowdene, London Road East. Evacuated to Amersham with her office who were based in Copperkins Lane.

Isaacs, Miss
Lent Marjorie Glover a hat. Untraced.

Jeans, Dr
James Hopwood Jeans, Cambridge.

Johns, Dr Samuel
Mabel's Doctor and the Bolams.
The practice was called Johns, Rolt & Strang, physicians and surgeons; The Firs, High Street, Amersham. It was a large house on the corner of Cherry Lane. The surgery was an annexe on the side of the house. Dr Johns was very *"old school"*.[5] The house was later owned by Ludovic Kennedy and Moira Shearer and renamed Piers Place.

Johnston, Frank
Grower of Russian Kale.
[unable to trace]

Juniper, Muriel 1906–2000
Artist and Book Illustrator. Assistant to Clare Leighton before the war. Member of the Women's International Art Club. Eric Newton was an advisor to the Club.

4 Bucks Herald. 20 April 1918.
5 Conversation with Godfrey Bolam.

Kent, Duke of 1902–1942
Prince George, Duke of Kent. Fourth son of King George V and Queen Mary. A Group Captain in the RAF during the war. He was killed when a flying boat in which he was a passenger hit a hill side in Scotland in bad weather. His funeral took place in St George's Chapel Windsor on 29 August 1942.

Keogh, Mab 1886–1935
Friend of Mabels and possibly a cousin. When she died in 1935 she left Mabel the residue of her estate.

Knight, Mrs
Rosegarth, Highland Road. Interviewed the Lewises with a view to them billeting there.

Knowles, Lucy 1870–1952
Lived in Welwyn Garden city. Mabel's cousin. Lucy went to Clara's 100th birthday party.

Larg, Dora
Worker at Friends House London on the Social Service Council.

Laski, Harold 1893–1950
Friend of H.N. Brailsford. British political theorist, economist, author and lecturer. Chairman of the British Labour Party 1945–1946.

Leighton, Clare 1898–1989
Artist and wood-block engraver, book illustrator and writer. She engraved an image of Bury Farm as the frontispiece for Mabel's book The Making of William Penn. She was effectively Mabel's sister-in-law.

Clare first met H.N. Brailsford when he was editor of The New Leader and he published her woodcuts. They became close companions but were unable to marry as his estranged wife refused to give him a divorce. They built a cottage called 'Four Hedges' in Monks Risborough and it was here she wrote and illustrated her renowned books on agricultural scenes. She also designed posters for London Transport in 1938, one of which is in the Amersham Museum collection. Her work was in demand in both Britain and America. In 1938 she made the decision to move to America, but didn't indicate to H.N. Brailsford and Mabel that she intended to stay for good. She left Britain with a suitcase, typewriter and paintbox, and became an American citizen in 1945. She was a Vice-President of the Society of American Graphic Art. Among her works there were 33 stained glass windows for the cathedral in Massachusetts. She died, unmarried, in November 1989 and is buried in Waterbury cemetery, Connecticut. Her work is held in collections such as The British Museum; Ashmolean Museum; Boston Fine Arts; and in the British Ambassador's residence in Washington D.C.

Lewis, Mr & Mrs
Greylands residents. Bombed out evacuees from London. They had a son living in Stamford Hill and another in the R.A.F. They left Greylands to move to a new billet on 24 August 1941, but still visited and wrote to Mabel after this date.

Lewis, Arthur
Lewis' son in the R.A.F. His address in 1942 was 1375611 Sgt Lewis, A. Sergeants' Mess, R.A.F. Romsey, Hants.

Library
In a room in Friends House. Staffed by volunteers. Bucks County Council provided the books.

Lief, Mr Stanley 1890–1962
Pioneer of Naturopathy. Founder of Champneys Nature Cure Resort at Tring. Osteopath and Naturopath.

Lilienfeld, Hendra 1900–1990
Hendra Porges-Lilienfeld, Mezzo-soprano. Born in Prague. Married James Lilienfeld, a member of London Stock Exchange in 1937. Telephone directories of that time show them resident in Maida Vale, but they are living in Amersham at the time of the journal. Possibly evacuees.

Lockwood, Mrs
Husband Ernest Lockwood. They lived at Pathside, Chestnut Close.

Maesky, M
Bust sculptured by Epstein.

Martins, The
H. Martin & Sons (Builders & Decorators) London Road West, on the corner of Station Road.

May, Richenda
Piano student. Lived in London. [unable to trace]

May, Gabrielle
This might be Richenda, whom Mabel has mis-remembered. [unable to trace]

Milburn, Gordon 1870–1973
Rev. R. Gordon Milburn, MA, Durris, Stubbs Wood. Born in 1870 to wealthy parents in South London he went to Trinity College, Oxford where he gained a BA in 1893 and an MA in 1897. He was ordained into the Church of England in 1898 and after working in several parishes in 1901 became a Tutor at Bishops College, Calcutta. He was made Vice-Principal in 1906 and remained there until 1913. He married Mary Myers in London in 1927. He lived at Durris, Stubbs Wood, Chesham Bois, from 1936 to 1973 when he died aged 103. Mary appears to have died in 1954 aged 85. He wrote several books on religious subjects and was an expert on Indian religions. His papers and manuscripts are held at the Bodleian Library at Oxford. During the war the Milburns gave lodgings to a Jewish refugee and his wife, Elias and Veza Canetti. Elias Canetti devotes a whole chapter to Mr Milburn in his book Party in the Blitz. Artist and refugee Marie-Louise Motesiczky, who lived in Chestnut Lane, Amersham, painted his portrait. There is a Research Fellowship in his name at the Faculty of Theology and Religion, University of Oxford.

Millicent
Resident of Amersham. [unable to trace]

Moreland, Ethel
At Mrs Crawshaw's Quaker funeral. Member of the Society of Friends. Wife of Harold Moreland, MBE, JP, a partner in Price Waterhouse in the City. They lived in Gerrards Cross, Buckinghamshire.

Dr Morley Davies, Arthur
D.Sc. F.G.S. Hon. F.R.G.S. 1869–1959
Lived at Arngrove, Station Road, Amersham. Writer, historian, District and County Councillor. He published Buckinghamshire (Cambridge Press, 1914) and The Hundreds of Buckinghamshire (Records of Bucks Vol. XV, Part 4 1950).

Motesiczky, Marie-Louise von
"Polish Countess" 1906–1996
Artist. Lived with her Mother, Henrietta, and their housekeeper, Marie Hauptmann, at 86 Chestnut Lane ('Cornerways'), Amersham, until around 1950. Born into a wealthy family in Vienna, she emigrated to Britain to escape the Nazi regime. She became a British citizen in 1948 and later moved back to Hampstead, where she had lived before the war. Her paintings are hanging in the National Portrait Gallery, the Tate and leading art galleries around the world.

Mung
[unable to trace]

Muriel
Resident of Amersham.
[unable to trace]

Nash, Miss Clarissa Rosa 1879–1972
Godfrey Bolam remembers her as a *"fairly short, dumpy figure. A dated – Victorian – look to her style of dress. Dark velvet always in evidence. She wore curious button-up boots (possibly orthopaedic). She used to appear from time to time and chat to my Mother [Emily Bolam] and had a wide circle of acquaintances. She was an entertaining chatterer notably reporting "auras" she had perceived in various locations in the Town."*
She lived in Old Amersham.

Newton, Stella 1901–2001
Mrs Pearce's daughter, Stella Mary Pearce. From the obituary in The Independent: Stella Mary Pearce, costume designer and dress historian: born London 17 April 1901; OBE 1976; married 1936 Eric Newton (died 1965); died London 18 May 2001.
After leaving school she became an actress, then discovered a talent for costume design, and during WW2 she and her husband, Eric Newton, toured Britain lecturing on art history and design for the extra-mural dept of Cambridge University. Later she was an adviser to the National Gallery, and founded a postgraduate course in the History of Dress at the Coultauld Institute of Art. After her 70th birthday she wrote many books on the history of fashion.

Newton, Eric 1893–1965
Mrs Pearce's son-in-law. Artist, art historian and critic. Art critic for the Manchester Guardian and the Sunday Times. Writer, lecturer and broadcaster. Mosaic artist. His European Painting and Sculpture (1941) remained a standard text into the 60s, as did War Through Artists' Eyes (1945). He was a household name in Britain in the 1950s, largely through BBC radio talks and The Critics. At the time that Mabel visited his house he was living at 3 Cumberland Gardens, WC1.

Noel's Lady
This is either his housekeeper, Mrs Pollak, or the lady that he married in 1944, Evamarie Perlmann. HNB and Evamarie met at a Conference he chaired in London in 1942 on German underground resistance. She was a young German refugee working as a medical aide in St. Ives, and at the end of the conference she asked a question. Next day they bumped into each other at a restaurant and were together for the rest of his life. Mabel briefly mentions this conference on November 23 1942.

Old Man of the Woods

Bearded. This might have been Bob Grace a WW1 veteran who suffered from Trench foot.

Pearce, Georgia 1870–1963

Piano teacher, pianist, writer and lecturer. Lived at the Music Studio Chestnut Close, Amersham. Georgiana Maria Hoby Pearce a concert pianist and descendant of one of Queen Elizabeth's Privy Councillors. She taught piano, and arranged, musical concerts in Amersham, until 1954 when she moved in to her daughter's London house and lived there until her death.

Polish Countess

See Moteszizscky.

Pollak, Mrs

Noel's housekeeper / billeted refugee.

Pooley, Henry

Great nephew of Clara Brailsford and second cousin of Mabel.

Powell, Mary 1625–1652

The poet, John Milton's, First Wife.

Queen Mary 1867–1953

Wife of King George V, Mother of King Edward VIII, and King George VI, Duke of Gloucester, and Duke of Kent. During the war she lived at Badminton House, Gloucestershire. In wartime it was her custom to instruct her chauffeur to stop for anyone in uniform. The surprised service personnel were then given a lift in the back of her Daimler to wherever she was headed and on arrival were presented with a medallion that bore her initials.

'Queer church'

The church Georgia Pearce attends. Order of the Cross. A religious fellowship founded in 1904 by John Todd Ferrier that fosters compassion, pacifism, vegetarianism and the creative arts.

Rector

Rector of St Mary's. Rev. Charles Edward Briggs, MA. (1873–1949). Rector of Amersham 1903–1945. Cricketer. Played six matches for Hampshire in 1900.

Reed, Mr

Unknown. Invited to Clara's 100th birthday party. Possibly connected with the Methodist Ministry.

Robinson, Dr

Piano lesson from Dr Ticciati and pupil of Mrs Pearce. This is probably Dr Harold Desmond Robinson who had a practice in Great Missenden, Buckinghamshire.

Robinson, Miss

Met on the station.
[unable to trace]

Rose, Miss

Former pupil of Ticciati. Lived in Camden Hill. Had a cottage on the Isle of Wight.

Scarlatti, Domenico 1685–1757

Italian composer.

Settlement Building

Possibly the Peabody Estate Settlement Building at Whitechapel which was bombed in 1940. George Peabody set up the charity in 1862 to fund housing projects for the *"poor and needy"*.

Silver, Millicent

Piano. Part of a Trio at the National Gallery

Sloley, Mr Robert Hugh

Lived at Instow, Hollybush Lane, Amersham. Mr Robert Hugh Sloley was born in Calcutta in 1848, and married in Kent in 1876. He was a chartered accountant who had his own practice in London. His eldest son Henry followed him into the business, but his second son, Robert, became a teacher in Lancashire. However Robert Jnr died in 1903 at the age of 23. His daughter died in Amersham in 1938, and his son Henry was living with him in 1941. It is probably Henry Sloley that is mentioned in the journal.

Smith, Miss

Preacher at the Methodist Chapel, High Street, Amersham

Sommer, Dr

Mabel helped Dr Grove with the translation of Dr Sommer's book. [unable to trace]

St. Bride's Church

Bombed out City of London church.

Steele, Mrs Mary [Steel]

Lived at Kenora, Chequers Hill, Amersham. Member of the Society of Friends. Helped in the library at the Meeting House in Whielden Street. Her husband, John, managed the waterworks.

Stubbings, Mr Eric Stephen George 1900–1973

Lived at Carmen, London Road East, Amersham. Mabel's next door neighbour. He married Elsie K. Hatch in Amersham in 1929. He was born in Coleshill, Bucks the son of Fred Stubbings the Headmaster of the Coleshill School, Organist, Choir Master, and local artist.

Susan

Mabel's dog, a West Highland Terrier.

Suter, Miss

Mabel's cousin Bertie was in possession of letters written by John Wesley and Dr Coke, a missionary. They had been passed down from a relative of the recipient who was her husband's stepmother. She asked Mabel's advice about a repository. These letters are now in the Lamplough Collection, Methodist Archives Centre, John Rylands Library, Manchester. Some have been published in The Letters of Dr. Thomas Coke, edited by John A. Vickers.

Tagore, Rabindranath

Bengali Poet, Writer and philosopher. Godfrey Bolam remembers his mother reading Tagore's poems. Being a Quaker she admired his pacifist ethos.

Thompson, Dorothy 1893–1961

Radio broadcaster. American Journalist. Anglophile. Described by Time magazine as the second most influential woman in America after Eleanor Roosevelt.

Thompson, Mr & Mrs

Quarrendon Mill Farm, London Road East, Amersham.

Ticciati, Francesco 1893–1949

Composer, conductor, pianist. Born in Italy he came to London to study at the Royal College of Music early in the 20th Century. In 1920 he married Maria Stierli in Marylebone, with whom he had his two children: Maive and Niso. It is presumed the marriage ended in divorce. In 1921 he played his own composition for piano and orchestra

at Sir Henry Wood's Promenade Concerts at Queens Hall (before the Proms moved to the Albert Hall). Sir Thomas Beecham conducted his oboe concerto in 1929 in London with Leon Coossens as the soloist. He continued to compose and perform throughout his life. He was evacuated from Maida Vale in 1939 and was billeted at Flint House, Woodside Road, Amersham, but later moved to the Studio in Chestnut Close where he composed, lectured and taught piano. He is buried in St Mary's churchyard, Amersham.

Ticciati, Niso Augusto 1924–1972

Francesco's son. Composer, and music teacher. He married in Oxford in 1949, and fathered two sons: Oliver and Robin. He married again in Marylebone in 1958, and fathered Simon and Jill. He settled in Ealing and taught cello and piano. The Musical Times obituary describes him as harpsichordist, composer, pianist and conductor. He published many compositions and scores for training young cellists, and some of these books are still in print today. He was the conductor of the Ealing Symphony Orchestra. His son, Oliver, had three children one of whom is the renowned Conductor, Robin Ticciati who made his Proms debut 31 August 2010 at the age of 27.

Ticciati, Maive

Francesco's daughter served in the W.A.A.Cs.

Tinker

Freda's dog.

Tory Uncle

This is thought to refer to Mr John Simmons of 'New Chilterns', Amersham Common. Mr and Mrs Simmons often held concerts at their home, but they are not mentioned by name in the journal. It is thought that Mabel gave him this nickname from a literary reference. He was the brother of Sir Percy Coleman Simmons, a Conservative member of the London County Council for the City of London from 1919 and chairman 1921–1922.

Toynbee Hall

A building in the East End of London from which runs a charity of the same name that aims to help to eradicate all forms of poverty. It was started in 1884 by Samuel and Henrietta Barnett. It was founded on the principles of volunteering, and continues to do so today. It has a continual programme of talks and events to bring poverty awareness to all levels of society.

Vanstone, Mr

Warden of Toynbee Hall.

Walter, John
Mabel is referring to George Walter. This was a name that Walter Goehr sometimes used. See Walter Goehr.

Warde, General
Mabel proprietarily calls him "our" but is that a reference to an Amersham or a British resident ? [unable to trace]

Webster Jones, Mr
Osteopath in Buckingham Gate, London.

Wege, Jas. Frederick
Mabel's Dentist. The practice was called Wege & MacGillivray, dental

surgeons, at Dunkerry, Hill Avenue, Amersham. The terraced building has now been demolished. His home was Westwood, Devonshire Avenue. He was still in practice in 1952. He had three children.

Wesley, Susanna 1669–1742
Mother of John and Charles Wesley. Mabel wrote her biography.

Wesley, Charles 1707–1788
Methodist preacher.
Mabel wrote his biography.

Wesley, John 1703–1791
Methodist preacher.
Mabel wrote his biography.

Winstanley, Gerrard 1609–1676
Leader of The Levellers a religious sect that fought for equality of land ownership. H.N. Brailsford's last book was about this oppressed group.

Windy Knowe
Wells, Somerset. Home of Mab Keogh. See Mabel Keogh.

Wolffe, Leonard 1880–1969
Spelt Woolf. English political theorist, author, publisher (Hogarth Press), and husband of Virginia Woolf. Friend of H.N. Brailsford.

Wood, Sir Henry
Founder of the Promenade Concerts.

Wylie, Mrs
Highway cottage London Road. She attended Friends Meetings occasionally. Godfrey Bolam described her as a rather frumpy and awkward. Mr Wylie was quiet and studious, who worked in Local Government. He might have been a billeting officer. He helped out at the Library.

Amersham Museum

Amersham Museum has a collection of over 1500 original documents, dating from the 17th century to the present day. They provide a rich and fascinating insight into the lives of local people at all levels of society. The collection includes personal letters and diaries, estate books and ledgers, sale prospectuses, programmes, pamphlets and leaflets. The museum has begun the process of digitising the collection so that it can be made available, in the museum and online, to a much wider audience.

Amersham Museum's volunteers undertake wide ranging and in-depth research into the history of the town and the museum's collection. This includes using resources, both in the museum and those available at local studies centres, to better understand and interpret the town's stories. It also includes drawing upon people's memories of the area, many of which are stored in the museum's extensive oral history collection.

If you would like to join the museum's volunteer research team, please get in touch:
info@amershammuseum.org

bibliography

Brailsford, Mabel Richmond. Padri Elliott of Faizabad.
A Service of Song.
Compiled by Mabel Richmond Brailsford and C.R. Tasker. 1907
Published by London. R. Culley "Choir" Series Services of Song, No.1.

Brailsford, Mabel Richmond.
Susanna Wesley, the Mother of Methodism. With a portrait. 1910
Published by C.H. Kelly, London. Series: Library of Methodist Biography.

Brailsford, Mabel Richmond. **Quaker Women, 1650–1690.** 1915
Published by Duckworth, London.

Brailsford, Mabel Richmond. **A Quaker from Cromwell's Army**. 1927
Published by The Swarthmore Press and MacMillan in New York.

Granet, Marcel. **Chinese Civilization 1930**
Translated by Mabel Richmond Brailsford.
Published by Kegan Paul, Trench, Trubner & Co. Ltd.

Brailsford, Mabel Richmond. **The Making of William Penn**.
With plates including a portrait.
Published by Longmans, Green & Co. Ltd. 1930

B Bonn, Moritz J. **The American Experiment**. 1933
Translated by Mabel Richmond Brailsford.
Published by George Allen & Unwin.

Pinnow, Hermann. **History of Germany** 1933
Translated from German by Mabel Richmond Brailsford.
Published by George Allen & Unwin.

Pinnow, Hermann. **History of Germany.** 1936
Translated from German by Mabel Richmond Brailsford.
Published by J. M. Dent.

Brailsford, Mabel Richmond.
Susanna Wesley. The Mother of Methodism. 1938
Published by Epworth.

Brailsford, Mabel Richmond. **A Tale of Two Brothers.**
John and Charles Wesley. With plates, including portraits. 1954
Published by Rupert Hart Davis and Oxford University Press.

Brailsford, Mabel Richmond. **William Penn, founder of Pennsylvania.**
With a portrait. 1944
Published by Friends' Home Service Committee. (ran to four editions)

Amersham Museum

Amersham Museum is part of a half-timbered Medieval hall house at 49, High Street in the centre of Amersham's historic High Street. Exhibits range from archaeological finds, the story of the Lollard Martyrs, local crafts of lace and straw plait making, to many aspects of local life, including reminders of the town's World War II activities such as barrage-balloon making. There is an extensive collection of photographs from Victorian times to the present day which can be viewed on a touch-screen. The well-stocked herb garden provides a relaxing area in which to sit down. There are many activities for children.

For information about opening times
and activities, please visit the website at –
www.AmershamMuseum.org
www.amershamhistory.info

You can contact the Curator by email at –
Curator@AmershamMuseum.org
or by phone on **01494 723700**